Over 100 delicious recipes:
Apples

Over 100 delicious recipes:
Apples

Martina Blank

Photography by Brigitte Sporrer
and Alena Hrbkova

Notes:

Eggs
If not otherwise stated, eggs used in these recipes are of medium size

Milk
If not otherwise stated, milk used in these recipes is whole milk (3.5 per cent fat content).

Poultry
Poultry should always be cooked right through before eating. You can tell if it is done by piercing it with a skewer. If the juices run out pink, then it is not ready and must be cooked for a longer time. If the juices are clear, then the bird is done.

Nuts
Some of these recipes contain nuts or nut oil. People who have allergies or who tend to be allergic should avoid eating these dishes.

Herbs
If not otherwise stated, these recipes call for fresh herbs. If you cannot obtain these, the amounts in the recipes can be replaced with half the quantity of dried herbs.

Alcohol
Some of the recipes in this book contain alcohol. Children and people who do not tolerate alcohol should abstain from eating these dishes.

The temperatures and cooking times in these recipes are based on using a conventional oven. If you are using a fan oven, please follow the instructions provided by the manufacturer.

Contents

Introduction   10

Starters, salads and soups   18

Main courses   42

Cakes and pastries   80

Desserts   102

Beverages and sauces   130

Index   153

Apple stories

Apples grow in abundance all over the world, so there is no apparent reason whythey should have a special significance amongst all the other fruits.

Nevertheless, this small, round fruit has managed to change the course of history and no other fruit is mentioned as often as the apple in the history books and literature of the world.

If Eve had not lured Adam into tasting the forbidden fruit, we might still be living happily and contentedly in Paradise. The apple precipitated the Fall of Man and has thus became the symbol of temptation.

Apples and love

This did not bother the poet, Johann Wolfgang von Goethe. He once wrote 'You can wax lyrical about roses, but you have to bite into the apple'. He was not the only one who came to see the apple as a symbol of love.

Even in ancient Greece it was the custom for a girl to throw an apple to a young man as a token of her love. This custom was later adopted by prostitutes to lure men into temptation. The reason might have been the 'erotic magic' the apple is supposed to contain, the reason why Nordic priests were forbidden to eat it.

In ancient Persia, on the other hand, a man was recommended to eat an apple before entering the bedchamber of his beloved. It was believed to increase male power.

The apple was treated more chastely in Central Europe. In rural areas it was used merely as an oracle of love. Young girls would put an apple under their pillow on Christmas Eve, hoping to dream of their future husband.

The fact that the divinely sweet 'fruit of Venus' (in astrology, apples are associated with Venus) was looked upon with a more sceptical eye by some is apparent in a folk superstition of bygone days. Washing or polishing the fruit was not necessary for reasons of hygiene, but it was done because people were convinced that evil spirits and demons inhabited the apple skin

Apples and politics

History does not only tell of apples of love and magic. The famous apple of discord should not be overlooked.

In Greek mythology, Eris, the goddess of Discord threw a golden apple into the assembly of the gods of Olympus, causing a fearful quarrel. which ultimately led to the Trojan War.

This was not the only time that an apple has played a significant role in political life. The famous imperial orb surmounted by a cross, carried by kings and queens as part of the royal regalia since the 12th century, symbolised the predominance of Christianity. The orb is believed to represent an apple, which is not surprising, because it was a main source of food in Central Europe at that time. More than 1000 kinds of apple were known and planted in Europe during this period. Most had been cultivated for centuries using complicated grafting methods originally developed by the eminent Roman naturalist Pliny the Elder(AD 23–70).

Apples and science

The apple continued to be scientifically significant, even if only coincidentally. In the summer of 1666, one of these wonderful fruits is believed to have fallen on Isaac Newton's head, causing the physicist to discover the law of gravity. From then on, Newton always used a falling apple to demonstrate this law.

Folk medicine also made pioneering discoveries with regard to the science of apples. Until recently, it was believed that apples could cure virtually everything, from stomachache to eye disease, from varicose veins to baldness. To what degree the placebo effect was responsible, there is no way of knowing. But as the saying goes, he who can heal is he who is right. Even today, the proverb 'An apple a day keeps the doctor away' is still in current use wherever English is spoken.

Apples and eternal youth

Nordic people believe that eternal youth and beauty will be bestowed upon those who eat apples. This cannot really be proved, but as is well-known, faith is capable of moving mountains. Today, nutritionists would at the very least confirm that an apple is a healthy fruit. Research has shown that, the apple is rich in vitamins, minerals, fruit acids, pectins and easily digested carbohydrates. It really should be on the menu more often.

Health and beauty with apples

Potassium, magnesium, copper, phosphorous, calcium and iodine are only a few of the 20 or more different essential minerals and trace elements found in apples. They are also rich in vitamins A and B and contain a smaller amount of vitamin E, which strengthens heart capacity and the nerves. Apples are also low in calories, containing only 58 kcal (230 joules) per 100 grams. Because of its high content of fructose and glucose, the apple is an excellent source of energy and very helpful in counteracting lack of concentration and fatigue. The minerals such as potassium and phosphorous and the fibre content also stimulate the peristaltic action of the intestines. Thanks to their mild laxative effect, supported by their sorbic acid and malic acid content, apples are good companions when on a slimming diet. In addition, the pectins swell considerably during digestion, absorbing toxic micro-organisms in the intestines which has a purifying and cleansing effect.

Apples are healthy

On average, the edible part of a medium-sized fresh apple of about 130 g/5 oz contains the following:

Vitamins

Carotin	0.1 mg
Folic acid	0.34 µg
Vitamin A	10.4 µg
Vitamin B6	0.1 µg
Vitamin C	15.6 µg
Vitamin E	0.6 µg

Minerals

Iron	0.6 mg
Calcium	9.1 mg
Potassium	187.2 mg
Magnesium	7.8 mg
Sodium	3.9 mg
Phosphorus	14.3 mg
Zinc	0.2 mg

Nutrients

Fibre	2.6 g
Protein	0.4 g
Fat	0.5 g
Kcal	67.5
Carbohydrates	14.9 g

Apples are always in season

Apples are divided into early, autumn and winter varieties. Early and autumn apples can be eaten directly from the tree, so to speak. Winter apples, on the other hand, need time to ripen completely, and they are also easy to store. Due to specially developed long-term storage techniques, it is possible to offer fresh apples to the consumer all year round. Of course, only apples without any sign of bruising or rot should be bought.

The different kinds of apples

Only about ten different kinds of apple are commonly sold, although there are over a thousand varieties altogether. The main criteria for cultivation today are storability, hardiness and resistance to disease and to damage in transit. However, in the country the old, sweet-smelling varieties can still sometimes be found. Windfalls are perfectly good for baking and cooking, as unripe apples contain a lot of fruit acid which contributes to the flavour.

The commonest apples are Jonagold, Russet, Elstar, Golden Delicious, Cox's Orange Pippin, Granny Smith and Red Delicious. The choice is important, since some apples are better suited to cooking or baking, while others are better for eating as they are. Some are too soft to cook, such as Red Delicious. Firm, tart apples such as the Bramley and Granny Smith are the best for cooking.

This apple cookery book contains a large selection of recipes ranging from the old-fashioned, traditional ways with apples to the newest and most modern. Here you will find delicious apple starters (appetizers) and salads, nutritious meals made with apples, hearty apple stews, sweet apple dishes, savoury meat dishes with apples, wonderful cakes and apple desserts, and last, but not least, some additional specialities including drinks made with apples. In short, there is something for every occasion and every taste, and, of course, for every purpose.

Perhaps there really is another reason for including apples in one's diet. Perhaps our ancestors weren't far wrong after all in believing that there is a seductive magic to this divine fruit. Maybe there are still some Adams today who would allow themselves to be tempted by Eve's apple. There is only one way to find out – try it yourself. We hope that preparing and enjoying these recipes will bring you pleasure.

EATING APPLES

Cox's Orange Pippin

This queen of apples was discovered in England in 1825 by Mr. R. Cox and it has been available since 1850.
Skin: this round apple has a rippled, marbled orange colour progressing to a brownish-red
Flesh: greenish to yellow, juicy, becoming pleasantly soft
Taste: aromatic, sweet and fruity, tangy and slightly tart
Harvest: middle to end of September
Ready to eat: October to March

Worcester

This early apple was raised in Swan Pool near the English city of Worcester in 1874. It is a delicious eating apple, but it does not keep well.
Skin: a bi-coloured apple, green to yellow on one side, red on the other
Flesh: fine, white
Taste: sweet, juicy, very pleasant and fragrant
Harvest: August to September
Ready to eat: late August to September

Ashmead Kernel

A russet apple with an irregular shape discovered by Dr. Ashmead of Gloucester in 1700. It keeps very well.
Skin: rough yellowish-brown
Flesh: firm, creamy white
Taste: aromatic, excellent flavour, sweet but tart
Harvest: October
Ready to eat: December to April

Elstar

This is a cross between Golden Delicious and Ingrid Marie, developed in Holland in 1955. It came on the market in Europe in 1972.
Skin: smooth and golden yellow turning to a bright crimson
Flesh: white to yellow, juicy and crisp
Taste: lightly tart, tangy and refreshing
Harvest: middle of September to beginning of October
Ready to eat: end of September to March

Golden Delicious

This large, rather 'tall' apple, tapering towards the base, is the world's number one choice. It was discovered by chance in 1890 in a private garden in West Virginia, United States and has been widely available since 1914.

Skin: when fully ripe, yellow to golden-yellow, and sometimes a light orange on the side facing the sun
Flesh: yellow to white, firm and crisp, juicy
Taste: fragrant, slightly tart, sweet and with lots of juice
Harvest: beginning to end of October
Ready to eat: November to July

Jonagold

A cross between Jonathan and Golden Delicious, it was created in the United States in 1943. It has been on the market since 1968. This apple is large, round and fairly tall. It is similar in size and shape to Golden Delicious.
Skin: greenish-yellow to a rich yellow, with the side facing the sun a bright orange, faded or rippled
Flesh: yellowish, juicy, soft

Taste: sweet and slightly tart, very fragrant, well-balanced, neither too sweet nor too sour
Harvest: end of September to middle of October
Ready to eat: October to March

COOKING (GREEN) APPLES

Russet
Said to have been discovered in Boskoop, Holland in 1856 as a fruit-bearing seedling rootstock
Skin: rough and matt, sprinkled with a cinnamon-coloured 'rust', usually faded orange to dark red
Flesh: yellow and juicy, fairly firm, becoming softer
Taste: tangy and tart, strong, fruity, refreshing and full-bodied, rich in vitamin C
Harvest: end of September to middle of October
Ready to eat: December to April

Bramley
The prime cooking (green) apple. It was developed by Mary Ann Brailsord in Nottingham between 1809 and 1813. The original tree still stands. A large apple, it usually weighs 200–250 g (about half a pound), but may be up to four times that. It keeps all year round.
Skin: pale green
Flesh: white, crisp and firm
Taste: quite sharp and tart

Harvest: October
Ready to eat: November to February

Edward VII
This late cooking (green) apple was introduced in Worcester in 1908 and named in honour of the King.
Skin: a bright green becoming yellow
Flesh: firm, pale yellow
Taste: very acid
Harvest: October
Ready to eat: December to April

Orleans Reinette
This cooking (green) apple, also a russet, was created in France in 1776. It has spread extensively and more than 100 synonyms for it are listed throughout the world.
Skin: very rough, characteristic russet skin
Flesh: firm, pale yellow
Taste: tart, aromatic
Harvest: October
Ready to eat: November to February

Starters, salads and soups

Apples are high in vitamins, minerals and trace elements but low on calories, making them an ideal basis for starters (appetizers), soups and salads. They combine well with other fruit (Chilled apple and red currant soup, page 39), with vegetables (Chicory with apples, page 36), cheese (Apple and cheese salad, page 31), fish (Apple and tuna salad, page 38), and poultry (Apple and chicken kebabs, page 27). Served hot or cold, these little dishes are a particularly nutritious prelude to a delicious meal.

Silly rascal

This cold collation is one of the standard fish dishes on the coasts of northern Europe. The nutritious combination of horseradish and apples strengthens the immune system which is important in the harsh climate of the north, and it is said to be a good preventive measure against colds. Grated horse-radish is available in shops, but if the root itself can be obtained and freshly grated, it has a more intense flavour.

8 fillets of salted herring

500 g/1 lb unsprayed apples

1 tablespoon horseradish

½ bay leaf

4 peppercorns

250 ml/8 fl oz (1 cup) sour cream

375 ml/12 fl oz (1½ cups) milk

❶ Wash and rinse the herring fillets and put in a bowl or deep dish.

❷ Wash the apples thoroughly, remove the cores and quarter. Grate the apples, put in a bowl and mix with the horseradish.

❸ Crush the bay leaf and the peppercorns, mix with the sour cream and the milk and add to the apple and horseradish mixture. Stir well.

❹ Pour over the herrings and serve with brown bread or toast.

Serves four, 450 kcal per serving.

Apple and fish dip with curried sticks

This light curry-flavoured dish is a good appetizer containing valuable protein. Curry paste includes turmeric and coriander, spices widely used in India for their positive balancing effect which encourages a feeling of well-being.

❶ Wash the smoked mackerel and remove the skin and bones. Put the fish in a blender with the cream cheese and curry powder and blend to a smooth consistency. Season with salt and pepper and put in a small bowl. Set aside.

❷ Peel the apples, remove the cores and quarter. Cut the quarters into thin slices and use them to garnish the mackerel paste. Put aside.

❸ Pre-heat the oven to 200°C (400°F), Gas Mark 6.

❹ Cut the crust off the slices of bread and put on a baking sheet. Mix the butter and the curry paste together well and spread on the slices of bread.

❺ Bake the pieces of bread for about 10 minutes until golden brown and crisp. Cut into sticks and serve with the dip.

Serves four, 480 kcal per serving.

350 g/12 oz smoked mackerel

150 g/5 oz cream cheese

½ teaspoon curry powder

salt

freshly ground black pepper

250 g/½ lb apples

4 slices of white bread

25 g/1 oz (2 tablespoons) softened butter

1 teaspoon Madras curry paste (from supermarkets or Asian shops)

Pitta bread with chicken and apple filling

This is healthy fast food for hectic days. The filled pieces of pitta are quick to make but they are full of valuable nutrients and vitamins. Originally from the Mediterranean region, this recipe is a great dish when you are pressed for time.

150 g/5 oz red apples

¼ red cabbage

2 radishes

1 small red onion

1 tablespoon lemon juice

3 tablespoons low-fat cream cheese

salt

freshly ground black pepper

200 g/7 oz cooked chicken breast without the skin

4 large (or 8 small) pieces of pitta bread

½ bunch parsley for garnishing

❶ Peel the apples, remove the core and quarter. Grate finely.

❷ Wash the red cabbage and radishes and cut into thin julienne strips. Peel the onion and cut into fine rings. Put all the ingredients in a large bowl and sprinkle with the lemon juice.

❸ Mix in the cream cheese and add salt and pepper to taste.

❹ Cut the chicken into bite-size pieces and add to the cabbage mixture.

❺ Bake the pitta bread according to instructions. Cut open on one side and fill with the apple, chicken and cabbage mixture.

❻ Wash the parsley, chop finely and garnish the filled pitta breads. Serve them while still hot.

Serves four, 310 kcal per serving.

Fried grated potatoes with apples

The humble fried potato can become interesting if combined with the right ingredients. This caramelised apple is an exotic variation for those who like to experiment.

❶ Wash the apples thoroughly, remove the cores and quarter. Dice small.

❷ Melt the butter over a medium heat. Add the diced apple and stir into the butter. Add lemon juice, sugar and cinnamon and simmer over a low heat, stirring continuously until the apples are soft and golden brown. Remove from the pan and put in a bowl.

❸ Peel the onion and chop finely. Wash and peel the potatoes, grate them with a cheese grater, put them in a clean tea towel and press out the liquid. Put the onions in a bowl with the potatoes and season with salt and pepper.

❹ Heat oil in a large frying pan. Carefully drop in spoonfuls of the potato and onion mixture, press flat and fry for about 6 minutes, turning occasionally. Remove from the pan and drain on kitchen paper.

❺ Wash parsley and chop fine.

❻ Place a tablespoonful of the caramelised apple mixture on each potato cake. Garnish with sour cream and parsley.

Serves four, 250 kcal per serving.

250 g/8 oz untreated eating apples
4 tablespoons butter
1 teaspoon lemon juice
1 teaspoon sugar
1 shake of cinnamon
½ onion
2 floury potatoes
salt
freshly ground black pepper
oil
½ bunch parsley for garnishing
50 ml/2 fl oz (¼ cup) sour cream

Prawn (shrimp) cocktail with apples

A delicious appetizer for those special evenings. At a dinner for two, this sophisticated dish can be served with a glass of fine champagne as an hors d'oeuvre. It stimulates the senses and sets the mood for the courses to follow.

350 g/12 oz apples

juice of 1 lemon

75 g/3 oz prawns (shrimps)

100 ml/3½ fl oz (scant ½ cup) sour cream

salt

freshly ground white pepper

1 sprinkle of sugar

2 tablespoons dill

20 ml/1 fl oz (2 tablespoons) white wine

1 tomato

❶ Peel the apples, remove the cores and quarter. Cut the quarters into fine slices. Sprinkle with lemon juice.

❷ Wash the prawns (shrimps), peel (shell) and clean. Bring 300 ml/10 fl oz (1¼ cups) water to the boil in a small saucepan, add the prawns (shrimps) and cook for 3 to 4 minutes.

❸ Remove the prawns (shrimps) from the water and drain. Mix the prawns (shrimps) with the marinated apple slices and spoon into cocktail glasses.

❹ For the sauce, mix the cream with salt, pepper, sugar and some dill, add the white wine and stir the whole until smooth.

❺ Wash the tomato, cut out the stalk end and slice into decorative thin strips. Pour the sauce over the prawn (shrimp) mixture and garnish with the dill and strips of tomato.

Serves four, 120 kcal per serving.

Apple and chicken kebabs

To save time, these tasty kebabs can also be made with a takeaway (carryout) roast chicken. Serve with cranberries and hot buttered toast.

❶ Wash the half chicken, rub with salt, pepper, paprika and curry powder. Heat two-thirds of the butter in a pan and fry the chicken for about 30 minutes until done. Add some hot water if necessary.

❷ Remove the meat from the carcass and dice coarsely.

❸ Peel the apples, remove the cores and quarter. Cut the quarters into large cubes.

❹ Push the chicken pieces and apple cubes alternately onto the skewers . Spread with the remaining butter. Stick the cherries onto the ends of the skewers and grill (broil) the kebabs under a pre-heated grill for 5 minutes.

Serves four, 280 kcal per serving.

½ roasting chicken

salt

freshly ground pepper

paprika powder

curry powder

60 g/2 oz (4 tablespoons) butter

400 g/14 oz apples

8 maraschino cherries

4 kebab skewers

Savoury apple kebabs

These light kebabs made with minced (ground) meat are ideal for a summer Sunday lunch or a small barbecue in the garden or on the terrace. They can be served then with rice or chips (French fries) and a tasty barbecue sauce.

1 small onion

125 g/4 oz (½ cup) steak tartare

125 g/4 oz (½ cup) minced (ground) meat, pork and beef mixed

1 small egg

1 tablespoon breadcrumbs

2 tablespoons raisins

salt

freshly ground white pepper

4 tablespoons oil

100 g/3½ oz piece of bacon

250 g/8 oz untreated apples

20 g/¾ oz (1½ tablespoons) butter

sugar

1 teaspoon sweet paprika

4 kebab skewers

❶ Peel the onion and chop finely. Mix in a bowl with the steak tartare, minced (ground) meat, egg, breadcrumbs and raisins. Season well with salt and pepper.

❷ Form the meat mixture into little balls, heat the oil in a frying pan and fry the meatballs for 5 minutes. Remove from pan and keep warm.

❸ Dice the bacon coarsely and fry in the hot pan until golden brown. Remove from the pan and keep warm.

❹ Wash the apples thoroughly, remove the cores and quarter. Cut a quarter of one apple into thin slices and set aside for decoration. Cut the rest of the apples into chunks. Heat the butter and a little sugar in a pan and sauté the apple cubes. Season with salt and paprika.

❺ Push the meatballs, bacon and apple cubes alternately onto the skewers and arrange on the plates. Garnish with slices of apple and sprinkle with lemon juice.

Serves four, 500 kcal per serving.

Power salad

This is a power food for fitness fans. The fruits and vegetables are just packed with vitamins, and the salad can be fitted into any dietary regime. The nutritious mixture of celeriac, apples and carrots supports the body's self-purification system.

❶ Wash and peel the carrots, then grate fairly finely. Peel the celeriac and grate that too.

❷ Peel the apples, remove the cores and quarter. Cut the quarters into thin slices, sprinkle with lemon juice and sugar.

❸ Cut two of the oranges in half and carefully remove the fruit flesh without damaging the skin halves. Peel the remaining oranges. Cut the flesh into small cubes.

❹ Mix all the ingredients together, add the sultanas and set aside to marinate for about 20 minutes. Fill the 4 orange skin halves with salad and leave to cool in the refrigerator.

Serves four, 210 kcal per serving.

500 g/1 lb carrots
100 g/3½ oz celeriac
250 g/8 oz apples
juice of 1 lemon
50 g/2 oz (¼ cup) brown sugar
4 oranges
50 g/2 oz (⅓ cup) sultanas

Apple and cheese salad

This is a traditional classic among apple salads and should always be present at a party buffet. The protein in the cheese makes this salad an important source of nutrients and energy. Served with a fresh, crusty baguette or ciabatta bread, it will also make a simple, light evening meal.

❶ For the dressing: mix the salad cream or mayonnaise, sour cream, lemon juice, vinegar, pepper, salt, sugar and dill in a bowl.

❷ Cut the cheese into cubes of 1 cm/½ in .

❸ Wash the apples thoroughly, remove the cores and quarter. Cut the quarters into fine slices. Carefully mix the cheese and apple slices together in a bowl.

❹ Chop the walnuts and sprinkle over the apple and cheese mixture. Serve the dressing in a separate bowl.

Serves four, 590 kcal per serving.

4 tablespoons salad cream or mayonnaise
125 ml/4 fl oz (½ cup) sour cream
juice of ½ lemon
2 tablespoons vinegar
freshly ground black pepper
salt
sugar
1 tablespoon chopped dill
300 g/10 oz hard cheese
400 g/14 oz untreated red apples
100 g/31/2 oz (1 cup) walnuts

One thousand and one nights salad

This is a very special delicacy reminiscent of magical oriental evenings. Redolent of the Orient, this appetizer is a wonderful hors d'oeuvre to have before an exotic main course. Serve it with an aperitif, such as a glass of prosecco with lychee liquor.

700 g/1½ lb untreated eating apples

juice of ½ lemon

175 g/6½ oz fresh dates

25 g/1 oz (2 tablespoons) white marzipan

1 teaspoon orange blossom water

4 tablespoons plain yoghurt

4 peeled almonds

4 fresh, green figs

❶ Wash the apples thoroughly, remove the cores and quarter. Cut the quarters into thin julienne strips. Sprinkle with the lemon juice.

❷ Wash the dates, cut in half and remove the stones. Cut into fine strips and mix together in a bowl with the apples.

❸ Put the marzipan, orange blossom water and yoghurt in a bowl and stir to a smooth paste.

❹ Pre-heat oven to 180°C (350°F), Gas Mark 4.

❺ Place the almonds on a baking tray and roast in the pre-heated oven until they are golden brown. Turn occasionally.

❻ Wash the figs, remove the stalks and cut a cross in the top. Press the lower half of the fruit together with thumb and finger to make it open up like a blossom.

❼ Arrange the apple and date mixture on four plates. Place a fig on each one, spoon the yoghurt and orange blossom filling into the middle of each fig, and decorate with a roast almond.

Serves four, 240 kcal per serving.

Fruit salad

This unusual, spicy apple salad with onions and sausages is a delicious appetizer. The Calvados, a French apple brandy, gives it a very special flavour.

2 onions
400 g/14 oz unsprayed apples
250 g/8 oz cooked pork sausage
1 tablespoon vinegar
1½ tablespoon Calvados
2 tablespoons oil
salt
1 pinch sugar
freshly ground pepper
½ head oak leaf lettuce
1 bunch chives

❶ Peel the onions and cut into fine rings. Wash the apples thoroughly, remove the cores and quarter. Cut the quarters into thin slices. Cut the sausage into rounds and then into small sticks. Mix everything together in a bowl.

❷ Put the vinegar, Calvados and oil into a bowl and mix thoroughly. Add the salt, sugar and pepper to taste. Pour the dressing over the apple and sausage mixture, stir carefully and set aside to marinate for an hour.

❸ Wash the lettuce. Arrange the clean leaves in a salad bowl and fill with the marinated apple and sausage.

❹ Wash the chives, snip finely and sprinkle over the salad.

Serves four, 310 kcal per serving.

Waldorf salad

The Waldorf salad is one of the most famous of all appetizers making use of apples. As its name suggests, it was created in the Waldorf Astoria Hotel in New York. It is now celebrated throughout the world.

❶ Peel the celeriac and cut into fine strips or grate. Sprinkle immediately with lemon juice . Peel the apples, remove the cores and quarter. Cut the quarters into strips or grate as well. Quarter the walnuts. Mix ingredients carefully together then, drain the pineapple chunks and add them.

❷ Mix the mayonnaise with the salt, sugar, pepper and Worcester sauce. Whip the cream and fold it into the mayonnaise mixture. Season and stir carefully into the salad.

Serves four, 330 kcal per serving.

¼ **celeriac**
2 **tablespoons lemon juice**
250 g/8 oz **apples**
50 g/2 oz (½ cup) **walnuts**
1 **tin of pineapple chunks**
4 **tablespoons mayonnaise**
salt
sugar
freshly ground white pepper
Worcester sauce
6 **tablespoons cream**

Chicory with apples

This chicory and apple salad is a light starter that goes well with meat or poultry dishes. It is a good idea to soak the chicory leaves briefly in warm water beforehand, to draw out some of the bitterness.

❶ Wash the chicory, cut in half and remove the core. Cut crossways into fine strips.

❷ Peel the apples, remove the cores and quarter. Grate the apples finely.

❸ Mix apples and chicory in a bowl, season with salt and sugar and sprinkle with lemon juice. Add cream to taste if desired.

Serves four, 130 kcal per serving.

6 chicory buds
700 g/1½ lb apples
salt
sugar
1 tablespoon lemon juice
cream

Apple and herring salad

This gourmet salad is said to help prevent hangovers, which may explain why it is often served at large banquets. It is also perfectly at home on any party buffet.

❶ Wash the herring fillets and soak in milk for four hours. Remove from the milk and cut into thin strips.

❷ Peel the celeriac and cut into thin sticks. Cut the gherkins into fine sticks too. Peel the apples, remove the cores and quarter. Cut into fine slices. Peel the onions and cut into fine rings. Mix everything carefully together in a bowl.

❸ For the sauce: Blend vinegar, oil, salt, paprika, mustard and cream in a blender to make a creamy liquid. Pour the dressing over the apple mixture and stir carefully. Refrigerate for 20 minutes before serving.

Serves four, 250 kcal per serving.

200 g/7 oz herring fillets
500 ml/17 fl oz (2¼ cups) milk
¼ celeriac
2 pickled gherkins
250 g/8 oz tart apples
2 onions
2 tablespoons vinegar
2 tablespoons oil
1 teaspoon salt
½ teaspoon paprika
1 teaspoon mustard
2 tablespoons cream

Apple and tuna salad

A simple but delicious salad that is quick to make. It can be a lifesaver when unexpected guests arrive, since the ingredients will usually already be in the larder.

2 tins tuna in oil

400 g/14 oz untreated apples

1 onion

½ head green lettuce

125 ml/4 fl oz (½ cup) plain
   yoghurt

juice of 1 lemon

sprinkling of sugar

salt

freshly ground pepper

❶ Drain the tuna in a sieve and break up with a fork.

❷ Wash the apples thoroughly, remove the cores and quarter. Cut into cubes.

❸ Peel the onion and cut into fine rings. Wash the lettuce, pat dry and divide the leaves between the four plates. Arrange the apples, tuna and onions on the lettuce leaves.

❹ For the sauce: Put the yoghurt in a bowl and season with the lemon juice, sugar, salt and pepper. Pour over the salad and serve.

Serves four, 350 kcal per serving.

Apple salad romantique

This apple starter is quite easy to prepare. It is particularly low in calories and is a good accompaniment to all diet dishes. Apples as starters have a similar effect to drinking an aperitif before a meal – they stimulate the digestive juices and so help to encourage good digestion.

400 g/14 oz apples

50 g/2 oz sugar

juice of 1 lemon

150 g/5 oz raisins

❶ Peel the apples, remove the cores and quarter. Cut the quarters into cubes.

❷ Put the apple cubes in a bowl and marinate with the sugar and the lemon juice.

❸ Add the raisins to the apples and add sugar and lemon juice to taste.

Serves four, 210 kcal per serving.

Chilled apple and redcurrant soup

This traditional recipe fits extremely well into the healthy wholefood cuisine of today, since rolled oats contain anti-stress vitamins. The soup is an ideal starter (appetizer) for people sitting down hungry at the table, because the carbohydrates satisfy voracious appetites, enabling the main course to be savoured more slowly.

❶ Stir the oats into the milk and leave to swell for 20 minutes.

❷ Wash the apples well, remove the cores and quarter. Grate finely.

❸ Add the lemon juice and the syrup or honey to the apples. Mix well.

❹ Stir the apple into the rolled oats. Refrigerate before serving.

Serves four, 220 kcal per serving.

75 g/3 oz (1 cup) rolled oats

250 ml/8 fl oz (1 cup) milk

600 g/1¼ lb untreated apples

juice of 1 lemon

60 ml/3 fl oz (6 tablespoons) redcurrant syrup or honey

Apple Lindau

This classic sweet apple recipe originated in the famous apple orchard region around Lake Constance in Switzerland. Being so rich it can even be served as a sweet main course.

❶ Cook the pudding rice following the instructions on the packet.

❷ Wash the apples thoroughly. Do not peel or core, but cut into large chunks. Bring 1 litre/1¾ pints (4½ cups) water to the boil in a saucepan and cook the apples and lemon peel until soft.

❸ Press the cooked apples through a sieve to obtain a fine consistency. Add sugar to taste.

❹ Heat the custard, add eggnog and fold into the apple sauce.

❺ Spoon 2 to 3 tablespoons of rice pudding onto each plate and pour the apple sauce over it.

Serves four, 330 kcal per serving.

80 g/3 oz (⅜ cup) pudding rice
650 g/1½ lb untreated apples
peel from 1 unsprayed lemon
sugar
250 ml/8 fl oz (1 cup) custard
4 tablespoons eggnog

Main courses

Thanks to modern storage methods, apples are available all the year round. This means that every season can be celebrated with meals using apples. As well as delicious sweet dishes (Apple Strudel, page 76), there are savoury ones using lamb (Lamb pie with apples, page 48), poultry (Guinea fowl with cider and apples, page 56), and many others, all illustrating the myriad possibilities of apples in cooking.

Pheasant à la Normande

This is a delicious, unusual way of preparing pheasant. The savoury, aromatic dish with cider, apples and cream is a particular delicacy for lovers of game. Pheasants can be bought from some butchers, fishmongers, supermarkets and occasionally directly from a gamekeeper.

1 pheasant, ready to cook

1 tablespoon olive oil

25 g/1 oz (2 tablespoons) butter

4 tablespoons Calvados

450 ml/15 fl oz (2 cups) dry cider

½ bunch parsley

½ bunch thyme

2 bay leaves

salt

freshly ground pepper

3 Cox's Orange Pippins

150 ml/5 fl oz (⅝ cup) double (heavy) cream

2 sprigs of thyme for garnishing

❶ Wash the pheasant. Using a sharp knife, cut into four pieces and remove the backbone.

❷ Pre-heat oven to 160°C (325°F), Gas Mark 3.

❸ Heat the oil and butter in a large casserole. Put in the pieces of pheasant and brown over a good heat. Pour the Calvados over the meat and flambé.

❹ Add the cider, parsley, thyme and bay leaves to the casserole. Season with salt and pepper. Bring quickly to the boil, remove from the heat and place in the oven with the lid on to cook gently for 50 minutes.

❺ Peel the apples, remove the cores and quarter. Cut the quarters into thick slices. When the cooking time is up, remove the casserole from the oven and add the apple slices. Simmer with the lid on for 5 to 10 more minutes. Remove the pheasant and apples from the casserole and put on a pre-heated dish and keep warm.

❻ Remove the bunches of herbs from the casserole. Bring the sauce to the boil and reduce by half. Lower the heat, stir in the double (heavy) cream and simmer for a further 2 to 3 minutes. Taste and season again if necessary. Wash the thyme sprigs and pull the little leaves off the stems. Pour the gravy over the pheasant and garnish with the thyme leaves.

Serves four, 540 kcal per serving.

Liver and apples

Liver with apples is an exquisite gourmet dish. Chicken livers can be used instead of ox liver. As well as being delicious, this is a very nutritious dish with essential vitamins and proteins. Remember to start the preparations the day before.

❶ Wash the liver and pat it dry. Pour the milk into a shallow dish and leave the liver to steep in it overnight.

❷ Remove the liver from the milk. Heat the oil in a frying pan and brown the liver on both sides.

❸ Peel the onions and cut into rings. Peel the apples and remove the cores carefully. Cut the apples into rings too. Add the apples and onions to the liver in the frying pan and sauté over a medium heat for 10 minutes.

❹ Wash the tomatoes, cut in half and cut out the stalk end. Add to the pan and cook. Season with salt and pepper. Serve with fluffy mashed potatoes or hot buttered toast.

Serves four, 360 kcal per serving.

800 g/1¾ lb ox liver

500 ml/17 fl oz (2¼ cups) milk

1 tablespoon oil

2 onions

400 g/14 oz apples

4 tomatoes

salt

freshly ground black pepper

Pork fillet (tenderloin) with apples

This is a hearty pork dish with a country touch. It is worth ordering a lean pork fillet (tenderloin) from your butcher a couple of days in advance. Ask the butcher to remove any fat. Serve with rice and a crisp green salad.

❶ Melt the butter in a large pan. Wash the meat and cut into bite-sized pieces. Brown over a high heat, remove from the pan and set aside.

❷ Peel and quarter the shallots, put in the hot pan and brown lightly. Add the lemon peel, cider and veal stock and cook all together for about 3 minutes. Add the pork and cook over a gentle heat for about 25 minutes until the meat is tender.

❸ Peel the apples, remove the cores and quarter. Cut the quarters into slices. Add to the meat and simmer for another 5 minutes.

❹ Wash the parsley, remove the stalks and chop finely.

❺ Remove the meat, onions and apples from the pan, arrange on hot plates and keep warm. Stir the parsley and the cream into the sauce in the pan and allow to cook a little. Season with salt and pepper and spoon over the meat.

Serves four, 560 kcal per serving.

25 g/1 oz (2 tablespoons) butter
500 g/1 lb pork fillet (tenderloin)
12 shallots
peel from ½ lemon
300 ml/10 fl oz (1¼ cups) dry cider
150 ml/5 fl oz (⅝ cup) veal stock
250 g/8 oz apples
½ bunch parsley
100 ml/3½ fl oz (scant ½ cup) cream
salt
freshly ground black pepper

Lamb pie with apples

A creative blend of lamb, apples and leek, best made with new season's lamb. The combination of the tender meat with the apples and leek inside a jacket of shortcrust pastry is a modern idea which is impressive and delicious.

1 onion

1 leek

150 g/5 oz untreated apples

675 g/1½ lb best end of neck of lamb

100 g/3½ oz mildly smoked ham

½ teaspoon allspice

½ teaspoon grated nutmeg

salt

freshly ground black pepper

5 sprigs thyme

150 ml/5 fl oz (⅝ cup) lamb stock

225 g/½ lb ready-made short-crust pastry

1 egg

❶ Peel the onions and slice into fine rings. Wash the leek and cut into thin rings. Wash the apples thoroughly, quarter, remove the cores and cut into slices. Wash the meat and cut into 12 equal pieces. Dice the ham.

❷ Make successive layers of meat, ham, onion, leek and apple slices in a large ovenproof casserole. Wash the thyme, pluck off the leaves and chop finely. Sprinkle each layer with herbs, spices and thyme. Pour the lamb stock over all.

❸ Pre-heat the oven to 200°C (400°F), Gas Mark 6.

❹ Roll out the ready-made pastry and lay it over the mixture. Whisk the egg and brush over the pastry.

❺ Bake the pie for 20 minutes. Reduce the heat to 180°C (350°F), Gas Mark 4, and bake for another 1 to 1¼ hours. If the pastry looks as if it is becoming too brown, cover with aluminium foil. Serve piping hot from the oven.

Serves four, 560 kcal per serving.

Pork chops with apple cream

The pork chops are simply fried in the pan and are therefore very quick to prepare. The sauce is made while they are cooking, so a hearty lunch can be ready in a matter of minutes. Serve with rice and parsley or with golden brown potato croquettes.

❶ Peel the apples, remove the cores and quarter. Cut into thin slices.

❷ Melt 2 tablespoons of butter in a pan. Add the apple slices and sauté while stirring. Pour in with wine and add the cinnamon.

❸ In a second pan, melt the remaining butter. Wash the pork chops and sprinkle with salt and pepper. Brown them quickly in the butter over a high heat, turning once. Reduce the heat and cook gently until done.

❹ Mix the crème fraîche with the apple mixture. Allow to cook until the apples disintegrate and season with pepper, salt and lemon juice. Serve with the pork chops in a separate dish.

Serves four, 600 kcal per serving.

250 g/½ lb apples

4 tablespoons butter

125 ml/4 fl oz (½ cup) dry white wine

sprinkling of cinnamon

8 pork chops

salt

freshly ground white pepper

8 tablespoons crème fraîche

1 to 2 tablespoons green pepper

1 teaspoon lemon juice

Apple and pork fillet (tenderloin) kebabs

Apples, sour cherries and pork fillet (tenderloin) make this recipe an extravagant delicacy for those who like surprises. The kebabs can be prepared indoors, wrapped in tinfoil and taken to a barbecue party to put on the grill.

❶ Mix the oil and apple juice in a bowl and season with nutmeg, garlic and cayenne pepper. Stir in the apple vinegar and the soy sauce. Peel the apples, remove the cores and quarter. Halve the apple quarters again and immediately add to the marinade .

❷ Wash the meat, pat dry and cut into slices 1 cm/½ in thick. Add to the marinade with the cherries and put in the refrigerator to steep for 2 to 3 hours.

❸ Remove meat, apples and cherries from the marinade and pat dry with a kitchen towel. Push in rotation onto the 4 skewers. Brush with the marinade.

❹ Pre-heat the oven to 200°C (400°F), Gas Mark 6.

❺ Put the kebabs on an oven tray, slide into the oven and bake for about 10 minutes to a golden brown. Turn and brush occasionally with the marinade. Take out of the oven, add salt and pepper and arrange on a serving platter.

Serves four, 410 kcal per serving.

250 ml/8 fl oz (1 cup) oil

125 ml/4 fl oz (1/2 cup) apple juice

pinch of grated nutmeg

½ teaspoon garlic powder

sprinkling of cayenne pepper

1 tablespoon apple vinegar

1 tablespoon soy sauce

400 g/14 oz apples

750 g/1½ lb pork fillet (tenderloin)

150 g/5 oz stoned (pitted) sour cherries

salt

freshly ground white pepper

4 shashlik skewers

Heavenly bed of apples

Raisins, apples and paprika make an unusual combination which tastes delicious. This country recipe with an exotic air is a perfect dish for a sociable evening.

2 onions
4 tablespoons butter
300 g/10 oz smoked sausage
400 g/14 oz apples
3 tablespoons raisins
3 tablespoons honey
paprika
salt
freshly ground pepper
1 sprig marjoram

❶ Melt 3 tablespoons butter in a pan. Peel the onions, cut into thin rings and sauté until transparent.

❷ Cut the smoked sausage into cubes, add to the onions and sauté also.

❸ Peel the apples, remove the cores and quarter. Cut into thick slices. Melt the remaining butter in a saucepan and cook the apples gently. Add raisins, honey and spices.

❹ Wash the marjoram, pluck off the leaves and chop finely. Put the apple mixture on a large platter, arrange the smoked sausage on it and sprinkle with marjoram.

Serves four, 440 kcal per serving.

Apple and cabbage pie

This is a recipe from Russia. Using frozen, ready-made puff pastry, it is an easy dish to prepare. The apples and cabbage are rich in vitamin C.

200 g/7 oz cabbage

150 g/5 oz untreated apples

50 g/2 oz piece of bacon

100 g/3½ oz onions

70 g/3 oz butter

500 g/1 lb frozen puff pastry

500 g/1 lb fillet of beef

6 tablespoons vegetable oil

salt

freshly ground pepper

❶ Wash the cabbage and cut the leaves into strips. Wash the apples thoroughly, remove the cores and quarter. Cut into fine wedges. Dice the bacon. Peel and chop the onions. Melt 50 g/2 oz (4 tablespoons) butter in a pan, add the onions and sauté.

❷ Thaw the pastry.

❸ Add the cabbage strips, apple wedges and bacon to the onions and sauté. Wash the meat, pat dry and cut into thin slices. Season with salt and pepper. Heat 3 tablespoons vegetable oil in a separate frying pan and brown the meat briefly on all sides over a medium heat.

❹ Grease a pie dish with the rest of the butter. Roll out the thawed pastry and use half to cover the bottom of the pie dish.

❺ Pre-heat oven to 180°C (350°F), Gas Mark 4.

❻ Alternately layer the cabbage mixture and the meat in the pie dish. Cover with the rest of the pastry. Bake the pie in the pre-heated oven for about 45 minutes. Test with a skewer to see if done.

Serves four, 1060 kcal per serving.

Baked apple with sauerkraut filling

This is an unusual but delicious variation of baked apple. It goes well with hearty dishes such as smoked pork rib and it is also a good accompaniment to grilled (broiled) pork sausages.

❶ Wash the apples thoroughly. Cut a small 'lid' off the top of each one and carefully cut out the core. Hollow out each apple a little.

❷ Crush the juniper berries. Finely chop the ham and sauerkraut. Put the juniper berries, paprika and 1 teaspoon crème fraîche in a bowl, mix in the sauerkraut and the ham and fill the apples with the mixture.

❸ Pre-heat oven to 200°C (400°F), Gas Mark 6.

❹ Pour the beer into an oven dish and place the apples in it. Put a dab of crème fraîche on top of the mixture in each apple. Replace the lids on the apples, put in the oven and bake for about 35 minutes until soft.

❺ Remove the apples from the dish, stir the remaining crème fraîche into the beer sauce and cook until it has reduces a little. Arrange the apples on plates and serve with the sauce.

Serves four, 290 kcal per serving.

500 g/1 lb untreated apples
4 juniper berries
60 g/2 oz raw sauerkraut
60 g/2 oz cooked ham
¼ teaspoon sweet paprika
150 g/5 oz crème fraîche
250 ml/8 fl oz (1 cup) beer

Guinea fowl with cider and apples

Guinea fowl has a much stronger flavour than chicken and the meat is darker. Served with apples and cider, this dish is a tasty alternative to game. Guinea fowl can be bought at some butchers and supermarkets. Buy a ready-drawn bird or have it drawn for you when you buy it.

1 guinea fowl ready to cook (plucked and drawn)

½ onion

2 teaspoons butter

salt

freshly ground black pepper

300 ml/10 fl oz (1¼ cups) dry cider

150 ml/5 fl oz (⅝ cup) chicken stock

2 sticks (stalks) celery

3 bay leaves

250 g/8 oz apples

4 tablespoons double (heavy) cream

several fresh sage leaves

½ bunch parsley

❶ Wash the fowl, pat dry and stuff with chopped onion and some butter. Put in a roasting tin, season with salt and pepper. Rub with butter.

❷ Pre-heat oven to 190°C (375°F), Gas Mark 5.

❸ Pour the cider and chicken stock over the bird and cover it with aluminium foil. Cook for about 1½ hours, basting occasionally with the stock.

❹ Meanwhile wash and cut up the celery, peel the apples, quarter and core them. Cut into slices. For the last 20 minutes of the cooking time, remove the tinfoil from the guinea fowl and baste again. Add the apples and celery. When the bird is done, remove to a heated dish and keep warm. Remove the apple and celery with a slotted spoon and set aside.

❺ Boil the liquid over a high heat until it is reduced to about 150 ml/5 fl oz (⅝ cup). Stir in the double (heavy) cream. Wash the sage leaves, finely chop half of them and add to the sauce. Taste and season as necessary. Allow to simmer for several minutes. Wash the parsley and chop finely. Return the apples and celery to the roasting tin with the parsley and re-heat. Garnish the guinea fowl with the sage and pour the sauce over it.

Serves four, 330 kcal per serving.

Apple chicken in puff pastry

A tasty chicken with an exquisite apple filling. This is a recipe for special occasions. It is very filling, so it may be served with just a crisp green salad.

❶ For the filling: Peel the apples, remove the cores and quarter. Cut the quarters into fine slices and put in a bowl. Pour over the apple schnapps and leave to steep for several hours.

❷ Mix together the curd (farmer's) cheese, the minced (ground) meat and 1 egg. Add to the marinated apple slices and season with salt and pepper.

❸ Pre-heat oven to 200°C (400°F), Gas Mark 6.

❹ Wash the chicken and pat dry. Stuff with the minced (ground) meat and apple mixture. Brush with oil and roast in the pre-heated oven for 30 to 40 minutes. Turn often and baste with the juices.

❺ Remove the chicken from the oven and leave to cool a little. Let the puff pastry thaw.

❻ Roll out the pastry, put the chicken on it and fold up over the bird. Leave a small opening at the top for the steam to escape. Separate the egg white from the yolk and set aside. Put the pastry-wrapped chicken on a greased baking sheet and brush with egg yolk.

❼ Bake for about 20 minutes. Test with a fork to see if done.

Serves four, 700 kcal per serving.

250 g/8 oz apples

400 ml/14 fl oz (1¾ cups) apple schnapps

1 packet frozen puff pastry

2 tablespoons curd (farmer's) cheese

150 g/5 oz minced (ground) meat, beef and pork mixed

2 eggs

salt

freshly ground pepper

1 chicken ready to cook

4 tablespoons oil

Apple pizza

Apples give this otherwise traditional pizza a special touch.
A full-bodied red wine is the perfect accompaniment.

❶ Sift the flour into a bowl. Make a hollow in the middle and crumble in the yeast. Sprinkle the sugar over it. Add 125 ml/4 fl oz (½ cup) water and knead to make a firm dough. Cover and leave to rise in a warm place for 10 minutes. Add the salt and brandy and knead well. Leave covered for 30 minutes more.

❷ Meanwhile, heat the olive oil in a saucepan. Add the tinned tomatoes and cook briefly. Peel and crush the garlic. Add the herbs and garlic to the tomatoes and cook to a smooth sauce over a high heat.

❸ Grease a baking sheet with the margarine. Knead the dough again, roll it out into a circle and lay it out on the sheet. Spread the tomato sauce over it.

❹ Cut the ham in strips. Peel the apples, carefully remove the cores and cut the apples into rings. Wash the tomatoes, cut out the stalk end and cut into slices. Peel the onions and cut into rings. Arrange the ham, apples, tomatoes and onions on the pizza dough and season with salt and pepper.

❺ Pre-heat the oven to 200°C (400°F), Gas Mark 6.

❻ Beat the egg, add the cheese and pour over the pizza. Bake in the pre-heated oven for 40 minutes. Remove from the oven and sprinkle with oregano.

Serves four, 530 kcal per serving.

150 g/5 oz wheat flour

10 g/⅜ oz (2 teaspoons) yeast

1 pinch sugar

1 pinch salt

1 tablespoon brandy

2 tablespoons olive oil

1 tin chopped tomatoes

1 clove garlic

¼ teaspoon dried thyme

¼ dried oregano

softened margarine for the baking sheet

250 g/8 oz cooked ham

600 g/1¼ lb apples

2 tomatoes

2 onions

salt

freshly ground white pepper

1 egg

100 g/3½ oz (scant 1 cup) Emmental cheese, grated

1 tablespoon dried oregano

Pork casserole with apples

This tasty casserole is inexpensive and makes a delicious lunch for the whole family. Pork is a good source of the B vitamins and should be on the menu often, particularly when life is stressful.

500 g/1 lb potatoes

salt

500 g/1 lb pork spare ribs

freshly ground black pepper

1 large onion

3 sticks (stalks) celery

5 to 6 sage leaves

½ bunch parsley

2 tablespoons sunflower oil

250 g/8 oz eating apples

150 ml/5 fl oz (⅝ cup) apple juice

150 ml/5 fl oz (⅝ cup) vegetable stock

1 tablespoon maize flour (cornmeal)

butter

❶ Wash and peel the potatoes and cut into slices. Bring a pot of water to the boil and parboil the potatoes for 8 to 10 minutes.

❷ Remove the meat from the bones, cut into even chunks and season with salt and pepper. Peel the onion and cut into thin rings. Wash the celery and cut up finely. Wash the herbs, remove the stalks and finely chop the leaves.

❸ Heat the oil in a pan. Sauté the onion rings and celery until golden brown. Put half these sautéed vegetables into another pan, add the cubes of meat and sprinkle with half the herbs.

❹ Pre-heat oven to 190°C (375°F), Gas Mark 5.

❺ Peel the apples, quarter and core. Cut the quarters into thin slices. Add the apple slices and the remaining onion, celery and herbs to the meat. Season with salt and pepper.

❻ Mix the apple juice with the vegetable stock and the maize flour (cornmeal) and pour over the meat and vegetables. Cover with the sliced potatoes. Melt the butter and brush over the potatoes. Bake covered for about 45 minutes. Remove the lid and brown for another 15 minutes.

Serves four, 400 kcal per serving.

Red cabbage with apples

This is a sweet-and-sour dish, with the mixture of red wine vinegar and sugar giving it a distinctive flavour. Served with potatoes or rice it makes a delicious vegetarian meal. Red cabbage is also a wonderful accompaniment to game or hearty pork dishes.

2 onions

250 g/½ lb eating apples

2 kg/4 lb red cabbage

2 tablespoons vegetable oil

4 tablespoons red wine vinegar

125 ml/4 fl oz (½ cup) red wine

2 tablespoons sugar

¼ teaspoon ground cloves

1 to 2 teaspoons mustard seed

50 g/2 oz (⅓ cup) raisins

salt

freshly ground black pepper

1 to 2 tablespoons redcurrant jelly

❶ Peel the onions and cut into fine rings. Peel the apples, quarter and core. Cut the quarters into fine slices. Wash and halve the red cabbage. Cut it into thin strips.

❷ Heat the vegetable oil in a heavy saucepan and sauté the onions over a medium heat until golden brown. Stir in the apples and sauté for another 2 to 3 minutes.

❸ Add the cabbage, red wine vinegar, red wine, sugar, cloves, mustard seed, raisins and spices. Bring slowly to the boil over a medium heat while stirring occasionally.

❹ Cover the saucepan and allow everything to simmer for 40 minutes until the cabbage is soft and the liquid has cooked away. Stir from time to time. If it gets too dry, add a little water. Stir in the redcurrant jelly just before serving.

Serves four, 320 kcal per serving.

Apple and vegetable stew

This is a hearty meal that is quick and easy to prepare. Sausages can be added if a more substantial dish is wanted. Cider or a dark beer go well with it.

❶ Peel the potatoes, wash and cut into large cubes. Peel the carrots and cut into slices. Peel the onions and cut into fine rings.

❷ Slice the bacon. Put it in a casserole with the potatoes, carrots and onions. Add the meat stock and cook everything for 15 minutes.

❸ Peel the apples, remove the cores and quarter. Chop into chunks. Add to the meat stock and cook for a further 10 minutes. Wash the thyme, pinch off the leaves and chop finely. Add to the stew and season with salt and pepper. Serve piping hot.

Serves four, 670 kcal per serving.

500 g/1 lb potatoes
250 g/8 oz carrots
3 onions
300 g/10 oz piece of bacon
250 ml/8 fl oz (1 cup) meat stock
500 g/1 lb apples
1 sprig thyme
salt
freshly ground white pepper

Curry risotto with apple

This dish is an example of fusion cuisine. Ingredients from more than one culture are combined to create delicious new taste sensations. In this recipe, the use of orange juice, curry and apples transform a traditional rice dish into a savoury, southern speciality with oriental overtones.

❶ Melt the margarine in a saucepan. Peel the onions, cut into rings and sweat in the margarine until transparent.

❷ Add the rice to the onions and stir until coated. Sauté. Sprinkle over the curry powder, pour in the broth and let everything simmer with the lid on for 15 minutes.

❸ Wash the apples, remove the cores and quarter. Cut the quarters into julienne sticks and put in a bowl. Pour over the lemon and orange juice and stir. Add the apples to the rice and cook over a gentle heat for 5 to 6 minutes.

❹ Wash the chervil, pluck off the leaves and chop finely. Serve the curry risotto onto plates and garnish with the chopped chervil.

Serves four, about 270 kcal per serving.

20 g/¾ oz margarine
2 onions
250 g/8 oz risotto rice
2 tablespoons curry powder
500 ml/17 fl oz (2¼ cups) broth
500 g/1 lb apples
2 tablespoons lemon juice
100 ml/3½ fl oz (scant ½ cup) orange juice
1 bunch chervil

Hare with apples

This is a special dish for the discriminating palate. Saddle of hare or rabbit makes a delicious meal. Buy the best and freshest meat you can afford for this recipe.

❶ Wipe the mushrooms with a kitchen towel, trim and cut into small pieces. Dice the bacon. Peel the onions and chop coarsely. Peel the apples, remove the cores and quarter. Cut the quarters in half again, lengthways.

❷ Season the saddles of hare with salt and pepper. Heat the oil in a large pan and brown the meat briefly on both sides. Remove from the pan and spread with mustard. Return to the pan.

❸ Add the diced bacon, onions, thyme and mushrooms and sauté everything over a good heat. Add the white wine, reduce heat and simmer for 20 minutes. Add the apples and simmer for a further 10 minutes.

❹ Remove the vegetables from the pan, arrange on heated plates and keep warm. Take the hare out of the pan, remove the meat from the carcass and arrange it over the vegetables.

❺ Bring the sauce to the boil to reduce it a little. Pour over the meat and vegetables just before serving.

Serves four, 380 kcal per serving.

250 g/8 oz mushrooms

50 g/2 oz piece of bacon

2 onions

500 g/1 lb apples

2 saddles of hare

salt

freshly ground pepper

2 tablespoons oil

2 teaspoons mustard

1 tablespoon dried thyme

250 ml/8 fl oz (1 cup) white wine

Hunters' apples

For this recipe you can use leftover game from another dish, or you can use fresh meat. A venison steak, for instance, could be cooked quickly in the pan before preparing the recipe. These stuffed apples make a light, tasty meal in themselves, but they can just as well be served as a starter (appetizer) or as a side dish.

❶ Wash the apples thoroughly. Cut off a 'lid', remove the cores and hollow out the apples a little. Cut the game into small pieces.

❷ Peel the celeriac and grate finely. Put in a bowl with the pieces of meat and mix with the cranberry jelly and mayonnaise.

❸ Fill the apples with the mixture and put the lids back on.

Serves four, 180 kcal per serving.

4 apples
200 g/7 oz cooked game
1 small celeriac
1 tablespoon cranberry jelly
1 tablespoon mayonnaise

Apple and onion quiche

This dish makes a delicious snack, or a light supper served with a fresh salad. Individual quiches can be reheated next day as needed.

❶ Grate 75 g/3 oz (¾ cup) of the cheese. Sift the flour into a bowl with a pinch of salt and ¼ teaspoon of mustard powder. Add the margarine and the grated cheese. Mix with 2 tablespoons of water and knead the ingredients together to a smooth dough. Refrigerate.

❷ For the filling: Peel the onions and chop small. Peel, quarter and core the apples. Grate the quarters finely. Heat 25 g/1 oz (2 tablespoons) of the butter in a saucepan and sauté the onions until transparent. Stir in the grated apples and cook for another 2 to 3 minutes. Remove the pan from the heat and let the apple mixture cool.

❸ Pre-heat oven to 200°C (400°F), Gas Mark 6.

❹ Grease a spring-form mould with the remaining butter. Take the dough out of the refrigerator, roll out with a rolling pin and line the spring-form mould. Leave in a cool place for 20 minutes, then bake in the pre-heated oven for 20 minutes.

❺ Wash the parsley and chop finely. Break the eggs into a bowl, add the double (heavy) cream, herbs, parsley, salt, the remaining mustard powder and some pepper and beat with a whisk until foaming. Grate 60 g/2 oz (½ cup) of the cheese and stir into the egg mixture. Cut the rest of the cheese into slices. Put the apple and onion mixture in the pre-baked pie case and pour the egg mixture over it. Arrange the cheese slices on top.

❻ Reduce the oven temperature to 190°C (375°F), Gas Mark 5, and bake the quiche for about 20 minutes until it is a beautiful golden colour.

Serves four, 850 kcal per serving.

190 g/7 oz Gruyère cheese

225 g/8 oz (2¼ cups) plain (all purpose) flour

salt

¾ teaspoon mustard powder

75 g/3 oz (6 tablepsoons) margarine

1 onion

400 g/14 oz eating apples

40 g/1½ oz (3 tablespoons) butter

2 to 3 eggs

150 ml/5 fl oz (⅝ cup) double (heavy) cream

1 teaspoon dried mixed herbs

½ bunch parsley

freshly ground black pepper

Apple pancakes (crepes)

These little pancakes (crepes) are perfect for hungry people with a sweet tooth. You can bake the pancakes (crepes) yourself, but if time is short they are also delicious made with frozen ready-made pancakes (crepes) from the supermarket.

350 g/12 oz apples

1 tablespoon butter

1 tablespoon flaked (slivered) almonds

cinnamon

1 egg

1 tablespoon flour

100 ml/3½ fl oz (scant ½ cup) cream

10 pancakes (crepes)

❶ Peel, quarter and core the apples. Cut the quarters into small pieces. Melt the butter in a pan and cook the apple pieces briefly. Add the almonds, season with cinnamon and sauté until brown. Remove the pan from the heat and allow to cool.

❷ Separate the egg and beat the egg white until it stands up in peaks. Sift the flour. Mix the cream with the egg yolk and gradually fold in the egg white and flour. Stir very carefully.

❸ Pre-heat the oven to 180°C (350°F), Gas Mark 4.

❹ Arrange the apple pieces on the pancakes (crepes). Spoon the cream and egg mixture on top and bake in the pre-heated oven for about 20 minutes.

Serves four, 300 kcal per serving.

Bean and apple hot-pot with smoked pork

This will be a popular dish for bean lovers. Beans are rich in protein and have a positive effect on the body generally. With the addition of smoked loin of pork and bacon, this makes a complete and hearty lunch, with the apples providing the vitamins.

100 g/3½ oz streaky bacon

500 g/1 lb smoked loin of pork

2 onions

500 g/1 lb green (snap) beans

20 g/¾ oz (1½ tablespoons) butter

1 clove garlic

1 teaspoon dried savory

freshly ground pepper

125 ml/4 fl oz (½ cup) apple juice

250 ml/8 fl oz (1 cup) vegetable stock

400 g/14 oz untreated apples

❶ Dice the bacon and cut the smoked meat into large cubes. Peel the onions and cut into fine rings. Wash the beans and top and tail them.

❷ Heat the butter in a large pan. Brown the bacon and meat evenly, add the onions and brown briefly together with the meat.

❸ Peel and crush the garlic. Add the beans, savory, pepper and garlic to the meat. Pour in the apple juice and the vegetable stock. Cook everything gently for 10 minutes over a medium heat.

❹ Wash the apples thoroughly, remove the cores and quarter. Cut them into slices. Add the apple slices to the pan with the meat and cook for a further 10 minutes. Check seasoning again before serving.

Serves four, 580 kcal per serving.

Duck with apple and potato gratin

This is an unusual delicacy, and the combination of apples and poultry is seldom featured on traditional menus. Serve it with a side dish of mangetout (snow peas), blanched for 1 minute.

❶ Score the fatty side of the duck breasts with a sharp knife. Season with salt and pepper. Heat the vegetable oil in a pan and brown the duck on both sides. Set aside and keep warm.

❷ Peel the potatoes, wash and cut into slices. Peel, quarter and core the apples. Cut them into slices too. Grease an ovenproof dish with the softened butter. Layer the apple and potato slices alternately in the dish.

❸ Pre-heat the oven to 220°C (425°F), Gas Mark 7.

❹ Bring the cream and apple juice gently to the boil and season with salt and cayenne pepper. Pour the hot apple juice over the potato and apple slices and cook in the pre-heated oven for about 15 minutes.

❺ Wash the extra apple, remove the cores and quarter. Cut into small pieces. Heat the margarine in a pan and cook the apple and the honey together. Add the Calvados and boil to reduce the sauce by half. Add the chicken stock and reduce by half once again. Thicken the sauce with a little arrowroot and pass through a fine sieve.

❻ Take the gratin out of the oven, arrange on plates with the duck breasts and serve with the sauce.

Serves four, 900 kcal per serving.

4 duck breasts (about 150 g/5 oz each)

salt

freshly ground pepper

3 tablespoons vegetable oil

500 g/1 lb potatoes

250 g/8 oz apples

softened butter for the casserole

250 ml/8 fl oz (1 cup) cream

250 ml/8 fl oz (1 cup) unfiltered apple juice

cayenne pepper

1 extra apple

1 tablespoon butter

1 teaspoon honey

2 tablespoons margarine

50 ml/2 fl oz (¼ cup) Calvados

500 ml/17 fl oz (2¼ cups) brown chicken stock

some arrowroot or cornflour (cornstarch)

Hamburger patties and apple gratin

It is easy to prepare this recipe in large quantities. It can then be cooked in more than one baking tin, re-heated next day or even frozen and cooked as needed at a later date.

1 onion

1 bunch parsley

500 g/1 lb minced (ground) meat, mixture of beef and pork

2 tablespoons curd (farmer's) cheese

1 egg

pinch of salt

freshly ground white pepper

1 tablespoon sweet paprika

sprinkling of cayenne pepper

3 tablespoons clarified butter

400 g/14 oz apples

softened butter for the baking tin

150 g/5 oz herb cheese

❶ Peel and finely chop the onions. Wash the parsley and chop it finely, too. Put the minced (ground) meat, onions, parsley, curd (farmer's) cheese, egg, salt, pepper, paprika and cayenne pepper in a bowl and knead together. Taste for seasoning.

❷ Make the meat mixture into little hamburger patties about 1 cm/½ in thick. Heat the clarified butter in a pan and fry the patties on both sides until they are golden brown.

❸ Wash the apples and carefully remove the cores. Cut the apples into slices 1 cm/½ in thick.

❹ Pre-heat oven to 200°C (400°F), Gas Mark 6.

❺ Grease a shallow, square baking tin. Arrange the patties and apple rings in the tin, overlapping them like roof tiles. Cut the curd cheese into little pieces and sprinkle over the top. Put in the pre-heated oven and bake for 20 minutes on the middle shelf.

Serves four, 520 kcal per serving.

Apple dumplings

This is a traditional dish from Eastern Europe. It was the custom to make sweet dumplings on Fridays, since in Catholic countries meat was not eaten on that day, and it was also a useful way of using up the week's leftovers. Boiled potatoes left over from the day can be mashed and added to the dough.

❶ Melt the butter in a small pan. Mix the flour, eggs, salt and milk or water in a bowl. Add the melted butter and stir with a wooden spoon until the dough pulls away from the sides of the bowl.

❷ Peel, quarter and core the apples. Cut into very small pieces or grate them. Add to the dough and stir in carefully.

❸ Bring a large saucepan of salted water to the boil. With a spoon, scoop out the dough into little dumplings and slide at once into the boiling water. Do not have too many in the water at once.

❹ Cook the dumplings for about 10 minutes. Remove from the water with a slotted spoon and drain well. Arrange on plates and garnish with butter, sugar and cinnamon.

Serves four, 620 kcal per serving.

1 tablespoon butter

500 g/1 lb (4½ cups) flour

2 eggs

salt

125 ml/4 fl oz (½ cup) milk or water

500 g/1 lb apples

butter for serving

sugar

cinnamon

Rice pudding with apples

This is a sweet pudding for everyone with a sweet tooth, and it is particularly popular with children. It can be served with apple sauce or another stewed fruit. Another variation is to include a layer of apple sauce in the pudding itself.

350 ml/12 fl oz (1½ cups) milk

150 g/6 oz (¾ cup) butter

375 g/13 oz (1¾ cups) pudding rice

2 kg apples

150 ml/5 fl oz (⅝ cup) white wine

125 g/4 oz (generous ½ cup) sugar

juice and peel from ½ unsprayed lemon

5 eggs

2 tablespoons rum

salt

softened margarine for the dish

1 teaspoon coarse sugar

cinnamon

butter for the top

❶ Heat the milk in a saucepan and melt 25 g/1 oz (2 tablespoons) of butter in it. Add the rice. Cook until the rice is done, remove it from the heat and let the rice cool.

❷ Peel the apples, cut in half and remove the cores. Heat 1 litre/1¾ pints (4½ cups) of water in a large saucepan, add the apple halves, white wine, 100 g/3½ oz (½ cup) of sugar and the lemon juice. Simmer until soft. Remove from the pan and drain well.

❸ Cut the lemon peel finely. Separate the eggs. Cream 125 g/5 oz (⅝ cup) butter in a mixing bowl, add the egg yolks, the rest of the sugar, rum, lemon peel, cooked rice and a pinch of salt. Beat the egg whites until they stand up in peaks and fold into the rice and egg mixture.

❹ Pre-heat oven to 180°C (350°F), Gas Mark 4.

❺ Grease an ovenproof dish. Spoon in half of the egg and rice mixture and cover with the apples. Add the remaining rice. Sprinkle the sugar, cinnamon and butter in flakes over the top and bake in the oven for 1 hour. Test with a skewer to see if it is done.

Serves four, 1250 kcal per serving

Sweet pancakes (crepes) with apples

This is a typical sweet dish from Austria and is a variation on sugared pancakes (crepes) with raisins. In Austria it is served with a glass of wine or cider.

❶ Separate the eggs. In a bowl, mix the flour with the egg yolks, 1 tablespoon of sugar and the milk and stir until smooth. Beat the egg whites stiffly and fold into the batter. Stir carefully.

❷ Peel, quarter and core the apples. Cut into small pieces. Add the rest of the sugar, the lemon peel and the rum and mix together carefully.

❸ Add the apples to the bowl of batter and mix thoroughly.

❹ Melt two tablespoons of butter in a large frying pan. Pour in the batter until the bottom of the pan is thickly covered. Brown the bottom of the pancake (crepe) slowly over a low to medium heat. Turn and brown the other side.

❺ In the pan, pull the pancake (crepe) into pieces with two forks and brown the pieces on all sides while stirring constantly. Remove from the pan and keep warm. Repeat steps 4 and 5 until all the batter has been used up.

❻ Arrange the pancake (crepe) pieces on a platter and sprinkle with the coarse sugar and cinnamon.

Serves four, 550 kcal per serving.

2 to 3 eggs

125 g/4 oz (1¼ cups) plain (all purpose) flour

2 tablespoons sugar

125 ml/4 fl oz (½ cup) milk

750 g/1½ lb apples

peel from 1 unsprayed lemon

1 tablespooon rum

100 g/3½ oz (1/2 cup) butter

coarse sugar

cinnamon

Apple Strudel

This is one of the most famous apple dishes and there are countless variations. This one is an old, traditional recipe. It is a delicious dish whether served hot with custard or cold with vanilla ice cream.

300 g/10 oz (3 cups) plain (all purpose) flour

pinch of salt

4 tablespoons oil

2 tablespoons margarine

50 g/2 oz (1 cup) breadcrumbs

125 g/4 oz (½ cup) sugar

1 kg/2¼ lb apples

3 tablespoons butter

1 teaspoon cinnamon

40 g/1½ oz chopped almonds

100 g/3½ oz (⅔ cup) currants

peel from ½ unsprayed lemon

butter

icing (confectioners') sugar

❶ Combine 250 g/8 oz flour, 125 ml/4 fl oz (½ cup) lukewarm water, salt and 2 tablespoons of oil in a large mixing bowl. Knead into a smooth dough. Form the dough into a ball, brush with oil and leave it to rest in a warm place for 30 minutes.

❷ Heat the margarine in a pan, add the breadcrumbs and brown them. Sprinkle with sugar. Peel the apples, remove the cores and quarter. Cut the quarters into thin slices.

❸ Dust a large cloth with flour, turn the dough onto it and roll out to a thickness of ½ cm/³⁄₁₆ in. Carefully stretch the dough by pulling all sides carefully with the hands until it is very thin.

❹ Pre-heat the oven to 180°C (350°F), Gas Mark 4.

❺ Grease a baking sheet with 2 tablespoons of butter. Sprinkle the breadcrumbs, apples, cinnamon, almonds, currants and lemon peel evenly over the dough. Using the cloth, roll up the strudel into a long 'log' and put it on the baking sheet. Brush with the remaining butter and bake in the pre-heated oven for just under an hour.

❻ Remove the strudel from the oven and dust with icing (confectioners') sugar.

Serves four, 980 kcal per serving.

Rolled fish with apples and vegetables

This fish recipe is light and easily digestible, but the smoked bacon and ham give it a hearty flavour. Serve with new potatoes and parsley and a glass of sparkling white wine.

4 cod fillets (200 g/7 oz)

2 tablespoons lemon juice

1 onion

50 g/2 oz streaky, smoked bacon

2 tablespoons butter

½ bunch each of parsley, dill and chives

salt

freshly ground white pepper

softened butter for the dish

1 tablespoon mustard

4 thin slices of smoked ham

550 g (1 lb 3 oz) apples

2 tablespoons white wine

sprinkling of sugar

1 tablespoon flour

4 tablespoons cream

3 teaspoons grated horseradish

2 tablespoons butter

❶ Wash the cod fillets, pat them dry and sprinkle with the lemon juice.

❷ Peel the onions and chop finely. Dice the bacon. Melt 1 tablespoon of butter in a frying pan and brown the onion and the bacon. Wash the herbs, chop the dill and parsley, and cut up the chives. Add to the onions and bacon and season with salt and pepper.

❸ Grease an ovenproof dish with the softened butter. Pre-heat oven to 225°C (425°F), Gas Mark 7.

❹ Salt the fish and spread with the mustard. Cover the fillets with the bacon mixture and roll them up. Wrap the smoked ham round them like a blanket and use toothpicks to keep it in place. Place the rolled fish in the buttered dish and cook for 20 minutes in the pre-heated oven.

❺ Peel, quarter and core the apples. Dice small. Heat the remaining butter in a pan and sauté the apples. Add the wine and the sugar and cook for 10 minutes over a medium heat.

❻ Remove the rolled fish from the dish and keep warm. Pour the liquor into a saucepan and add 250 ml/8 fl oz (1 cup) of water. Bring to the boil. Beat the flour into the cream, stir it into the liquor and simmer for 5 minutes. Remove the saucepan from the stove. Add horseradish and apples. Mix everything together carefully. Spoon the apple mixture onto four plates and arrange the rolled fish on top.

Serves four, 400 kcal per serving.

Squid kebabs with apple sauce

Squid is mainly familiar in its deep-fried form, but this marine delicacy from the sea tastes wonderful when it is just sautéed. The apple sauce is a welcome alternative to the mayonnaise usually served with squid.

❶ Peel, quarter and core the apples. Chop into small pieces, reserving four slices as a garnish. Put the apples in a saucepan. Add the sugar, lemon juice and apple juice, bring to the boil and simmer for 10 minutes.

❷ Peel the shallots and garlic. Wash and prepare the leek. Dice everything and add to the apples in the saucepan.

❸ Wash the thyme, tarragon and rosemary. Pour the vegetable stock over the apples and leek, add the herbs and boil to reduce to about half. Reduce the heat and keep warm.

❹ Wash the squid under running water, pat dry and thread onto the skewers. Season with salt and pepper. Heat the clarified butter in a frying pan and fry the kebabs, turning them so that they brown evenly. In a separate pan, melt the butter and sauté the reserved apple slices.

❺ Take the herbs out of the saucepan. Stir cream into the sauce and taste again for seasoning. Arrange the squid kebabs on plates with the apple slices and pour the sauce over them.

Serves four, 300 kcal per serving.

250 g/8 oz apples

1 tablespoon sugar

juice of 2 lemons

100 ml/3½ fl oz (scant ½ cup) apple juice

2 shallots

1 clove garlic

1 leek

500 ml/17 fl oz (2¼ cups) vegetable stock

1 sprig each thyme, tarragon and rosemary

500 g/1 lb squid ready to cook

1 tablespoon clarified butter

salt

freshly ground pepper

1 tablespoon butter

125 ml/4 fl oz (½ cup) cream

8 wooden skewers

Cakes and pastries

About ten different kinds of apple are commonly available, and a further ten or so varieties may sometimes be found. The flavours range from sour or tart, to sweet and aromatic or mild and fragrant, while the flesh itself may be juicy, soft, firm or crisp. Wonderful cakes (Quick apple cake, page 85) and delicious pastries (Apple Chelsea, page 97) can be quickly and easily made using all these apple varieties. Somewhat more elaborate, but well worth the time it takes to prepare, is Apple amaretto tart (page 91).

French apple tart

This is a wholewheat variation of the French national dish. When the French get together for a celebration, apple tart is an important part of the proceedings. It is served with the coffee after a hearty meal. Even in cafés small versions will be found as a sweet snack to accompany café au lait.

200 g/7 oz wholewheat flour

100 g/3½ oz (2 cups) butter

50 g/2 oz (¼ cup) sugar

1 egg

pinch of salt

1 kg/2¼ lb apples

2 tablespoons sugar

cinnamon

200 ml/7 fl oz (⅞ cup) Calvados

70 g/3 oz (¾ cup) chopped
   hazelnuts (filberts)

softened butter for the dish

2 tablespoons flour

2 tablespoons breadcrumbs

200 g/7 oz marzipan

1 sachet vanilla sugar

1 egg yolk

2 tablespoons apricot jam (jelly)

❶ Sift the flour onto a board and make a hollow in the centre. Cut the butter into little cubes. Put the sugar, egg and salt into the hollow, add the butter and mix everything together, kneading to a smooth dough. Wrap in foil and put in the refrigerator for half an hour.

❷ Peel, quarter and core the apples and cut into large pieces. Put on the stove in a large saucepan with the sugar, cinnamon, Calvados and hazelnuts (filberts) and cook gently over a low heat until soft.

❸ Pre-heat oven to 180°C (350°F), Gas Mark 4.

❹ Roll out the dough to match the size of the flan tin being used. Grease the tin with the softened butter and dust with flour. Lay the dough into the tin and cut off the overhanging edges. Press down into the corners and prick the bottom in several places with a fork. Bake in the oven for about 12 to 15 minutes, then remove from the oven. Sprinkle the breadcrumbs onto the pie crust and spoon in the apple mixture, making sure it is of even depth. Reduce the heat to 175°C (340°F), Gas Mark 3.

❺ To make the glaze, mix the marzipan with the vanilla sugar and egg yolk to a thick paste. Put in a piping (decorators') bag with a nozzle. Apply to the tart in a lattice pattern. Return the tart to the oven and bake to a golden yellow.

❻ Remove the tart from the oven and leave to cool. Bring the apricot jam (jelly) to the boil with 1 tablespoon of water. Remove the tart from the flan tin and glaze with the jam (jelly).

Makes 12 pieces, 340 kcal per piece.

Rhubarb and apple pie

This apple pie recipe using shortcrust pastry is simple but exquisite. Like 'Apfelstrudel', it can also be served hot. Eaten with vanilla ice cream, it is a hot and cold delight.

250 g/8 oz tart apples

400 g/14 oz rhubarb

100 g/3½ oz (½ cup) sugar

150 g/5 oz (1½ cups) plain (all purpose) flour

100 g/3½ oz (½ cup) butter

pinch of salt

2 tablespoons coarse sugar

❶ Peel, quarter and core the apples. Cut the quarters into thin slices. Wash the rhubarb, peel and cut into 2 cm/¾ in pieces. Sprinkle with half the sugar. Mix the apples and the rhubarb together and put in a shallow oven-proof dish.

❷ Sift the flour onto a board and make a hollow in the middle. Cut the butter into little cubes and sprinkle around the edge. Put the rest of the sugar and the salt in the hollow and knead everything to a smooth dough. Wrap the dough in a tea towel and refrigerate for 30 minutes.

❸ Pre-heat oven to 200°C (400°F), Gas Mark 6.

❹ Rewove the dough from the refrigerator and knead once more. Roll out thinly and cut into narrow strips. Arrange the strips in a lattice pattern on top of the fruit. Bake for 10 minutes in the pre-heated oven.

❺ Remove from the oven and sprinkle the coarse sugar over the pie. Return to the oven and bake for a further 20 minutes. Test with a skewer to check when it is done . Serve hot.

Makes 12 pieces, 160 kcal per piece.

Quick apple cake

A lightningfast recipe, ideal if you have to bake a cake in a hurry. The apples are simply pressed into the dough. This not only saves time – it also looks very decorative. After all, it should look as good as it tastes.

❶ Peel the apples, cut in half and remove the cores. Score the outside several times and put in a bowl. Sprinkle with sugar and 1 tablespoon of lemon juice.

❷ Separate the eggs. Cream 60 g/2 oz (4 tablespoons) of butter and the sugar in a bowl. Gradually add the egg yolk, lemon peel and the rest of the lemon juice and mix everything until it is fluffy.

❸ Sift the flour and baking powder together. Alternating with the milk, gradually mix into the butter mixture. Add the rum. Beat the egg whites stiffly and fold carefully into the batter.

❹ Grease a spring-form mould with the softened margarine. Pre-heat oven to 180°C (350°F), Gas Mark 4.

❺ Pour the batter into the spring-form mould. Melt the remaining butter in a small pan. Press the apples, core side down, into the dough and brush with the melted butter. Bake the cake for about 35 to 40 minutes. Test with a skewer to check when it is done.

❻ Remove the cake from the spring-form mould, leave to cool on a wire rack and dust with icing (confectioners') sugar.

Makes 12 pieces, 260 kcal per piece.

750 g/3 lb apples

juice of two lemons

75 g/3 oz (⅓ cup) sugar

softened margarine for the
   spring-form mould

2 eggs

80 g/3 oz (6 tablespoons) butter

150 g/5 oz (⅔ cup) sugar

peel from ½ unsprayed lemon

200 g/7 oz (2 cups) plain (all
   purpose) flour

½ sachet baking powder

125 ml/4 fl oz (½ cup) milk

1 tablespoon rum

icing (confectioners') sugar

Submerged apple cake

This is an easy and tasty cake. If you add cinnamon, currants or almonds, it makes a perfect accompaniment to afternoon tea.

300 g/10 oz (3 cups) plain (all purpose) flour

½ teaspoon baking powder

3 eggs

200 g/7 oz (scant 1 cup) sugar

150 g/5 oz (5/8 cup) butter

500 g/1 lb apples

juice of 1 lemon

softened butter for the spring-form mould

½ teaspoon cinnamon

❶ Sift the flour and baking powder into a large bowl. Add the eggs, sugar and butter and mix everything well.

❷ Peel the apples, cut in half and remove the cores. Sprinkle the halves with lemon juice and cut into fan shapes.

❸ Pre-heat oven to 160°C (325°F), Gas Mark 3.

❹ Grease a spring-form mould with the softened butter and scoop in the batter. Arrange the fan-shaped apple pieces on the top and sprinkle with cinnamon.

❺ Put the cake in the oven and bake for 1 hour. Test with a skewer to check when it is done . Remove from the oven and leave to cool on a wire rack.

Makes 12 pieces, 300 kcal per piece.

Glazed apple tart

A traditional classic among apple tart recipes. What makes this something out of the ordinary is the special glaze that covers the fruit.

125 g/4 oz (½ cup) butter

peel from ½ unsprayed lemon

100 g/3½ oz (scant ½ cup) sugar

2 eggs

2 tablespoons cornflour (cornstarch)

125 g/4 oz (1¼ cup) plain (all purpose) flour

1 teaspoon baking powder

600 g/1¼ lb apples

softened butter for the spring-form mould

50 g/2 oz (⅜ cup) chopped almonds

For the glaze:

2 eggs

100 g/3½ oz (scant ½ cup) sugar

2 tablespoons cornflour (cornstarch)

2 tablespoons plain (all purpose) flour

½ teaspoon baking powder

½ teaspoon cinnamon

icing (confectioners') sugar

❶ Put the butter in a mixing bowl. Add lemon peel, sugar and the 2 eggs and mix until foamy. Sift the cornflour (cornstarch), flour and baking powder over the butter and egg mixture and fold in carefully.

❷ Peel, quarter and core the apples. Grease a spring-form mould with the softened butter. Put in the dough and sprinkle with the almonds. Arrange the apples in a circular pattern on top of the dough.

❸ For the glaze: Separate two eggs. Mix the egg whites with one tablespoon of water and beat until stiff. Carefully stir in the sugar. Beat the egg yolk and fold into the egg white. Sift the cornflour (cornstarch), flour, baking powder and cinnamon into a bowl and mix together. Add to the eggs, folding in carefully.

❹ Pre-heat oven to 180°C (350°F), Gas Mark 4.

❺ Pour the glaze over the apples and bake on the middle shelf of the oven for 75 minutes. Test with a skewer to check when it is done. Remove from the oven and leave to cool on a wire rack. When cool, dust the tart with icing (confectioners') sugar.

Makes 12 pieces, 300 kcal per piece.

American upside-down cake

On the east coast of the United States, this upside-down cake with apple rings is a popular dessert on occasions such as Thanksgiving. It is often served with lots of whipped cream.

❶ Line a spring-form mould with baking parchment. Melt 40 g/1½ oz (3 tablespoons) of the butter and pour evenly onto the paper. Sprinkle 90 g/3½ oz (scant ½ cup) sugar over the butter.

❷ Peel the apples and remove the cores, leaving the apples in one piece. Cut the apples into thick slices. Place in the spring-form mould and sprinkle with 2 tablespoons of the lemon juice. Chop the walnuts and sprinkle over the apple slices.

❸ In a mixing bowl, cream the remaining butter with the sugar. Sift the cornflour (cornstarch), flour and baking powder and mix into the butter alternately with the eggs, the remaining lemon juice and the milk.

❹ Pre-heat the oven to 200°C (400°F), Gas Mark 6.

❺ Pour the batter on top of the apples, smooth the top with a spatula and bake in the oven for 10 minutes on the middle shelf. Test with a skewer to see if it is done.

❻ Take the cake out of the oven and allow to cool in the spring-form mould. Turn out upside-down onto a wire rack and remove the paper.

Makes 12 pieces, 300 kcal per piece.

120 g/5 oz (⅝ cup) butter

250 g/8 oz (1 cup) sugar

750 g/1½ lb apples

3 tablespoons lemon juice

75 g/3 oz (¾ cup) walnuts

80 g/3 oz (scant 1 cup) plain (all purpose) flour

100 g/3½ oz (¾ cup) cornflour (cornstarch)

1 teaspoon baking powder

2 eggs

10 ml/½ fl oz (1 tablespoon) milk

Hidden apple cake

This is another possibility for those who are pressed for time. In this recipe, the apples sink down into the dough and cannot be seen. Hence the name. Hidden apple cake is an excellent choice for taking on picnics as it keeps its shape.

❶ Separate the eggs. Cream the butter, the egg yolks and the sugar in a bowl. Beat the egg whites until stiff and fold into the butter and egg yolk mixture.

❷ Mix the flour, baking powder, salt, milk and lemon zest in another bowl, add to the eggs and stir in carefully.

❸ Grease the spring-form mould with the softened butter. Put in the dough.

❹ Pre-heat oven to 180°C (350°F), Gas Mark 4.

❺ Peel the apples, cut into eighths and remove the cores. Scatter the almond flakes onto a baking sheet and roast in the oven until golden brown. Turn often. Remove from oven and leave to cool.

❻ Spread the apples, currants and almonds on the dough. Dot with butter and sprinkle with sugar.

❼ Bake the cake for 30 minutes on the middle shelf of the oven. Test with a skewer to see if it is done. Remove from oven and leave to cool on a wire rack.

Makes 12 pieces, 200 kcal per piece.

2 eggs

75 g/3 oz (6 tablespoons) butter

75 g/3 oz (⅓ cup) sugar

125 g/4 oz (1¼ cups) plain (all purpose) flour

½ sachet baking powder

pinch of salt

3 tablespoons milk

1 tablespoon lemon zest

softened butter for the spring-form mould

500 g/1 lb apples

50 g/2 oz flaked (slivered) almonds

20 g/¾ oz (1½ tablepsoons) currants

20 g/¾ oz (1½ tablespoons) butter

30 g/1 oz (2 tablespoons) sugar

Apple amaretto tart

This is a delicious wholewheat tart with a very professional touch. It is somewhat time-consuming but is certainly worth it. Even a pastrycook couldn't make it better. For a particularly festive look, decorate it with hundreds and thousands.

❶ Mix the butter, sugar, vanilla sugar, rum and the eggs in a bowl until foamy. Mix the flour with the baking powder and cinnamon. Add the flour to the butter mixture and stir in well.

❷ Peel the apples, remove the cores and quarter. Grease the spring-form mould with the softened butter and sprinkle with the ground almonds. Fill with the batter and arrange the apples on top.

❸ Pre-heat oven to 180°C (350°F), Gas Mark 4.

❹ For the meringue: Add salt to the egg whites and beat until they form stiff peaks. Sift the icing (confectioners') sugar and sprinkle over the egg whites. Stir constantly until the consistency is shiny and firm.

❺ Fold the ground almonds, cinnamon and amaretto carefully into the meringue. Distribute evenly over the layer of apples. Cover the cake with aluminium foil, put in the oven and bake for 35 minutes. Remove the foil and bake for a further 15 minutes. Test with a skewer to see if it is done.

❻ Remove from the oven. Take the cake out of the spring-form mould and leave to cool on a wire rack.

❼ Prepare the gelatine according to the instructions on the packet. Whip the cream and add the cool, liquid gelatine while stirring constantly. Refrigerate. When cool, spread on the cake. Just before serving sprinkle with cinnamon or hundreds and thousands.

Makes 12 pieces, 450 kcal per piece.

100 g/3½ oz (½ cup) butter

100 g/3½ oz (½ cup) sugar

1 sachet vanilla sugar

1 tablespoon ground almonds

2 eggs

150 g/5 oz (1½ cups) wholewheat flour

1 teaspoon baking powder

1 teaspoon cinnamon

3 tablespoons rum

250 g/8 oz apples

softened butter for the spring-form mould

For the meringue:

2 egg whites

pinch of salt

200 g/7 oz (1⅛ cups) icing (confectioners') sugar

200 g/7 oz (1½ cups) ground almonds

2 teaspoons cinnamon

400 ml/14 fl oz (1¾ cups) amaretto

3 leaves white gelatine

400 ml/14 fl oz (1¾ cups) cream

sprinkling of cinnamon

hundreds and thousands, optional

Apple crumble

This apple crumble is a simple yeast cake cooked on a baking sheet, just right for afternoon tea. A good helping of whipped cream turns it into a delicious dessert.

❶ For the dough: Sift 350 g/12 oz (3¼ cups) flour into a mixing bowl. Press a hollow into the middle. Crumble in the yeast and sprinkle on 20 g/¾ oz (¾ tablespoon) sugar. Add the milk, stir together and then knead to a smooth dough. Allow to rest for 15 minutes, covered.

❷ Melt the butter in a saucepan. Add the butter, 30 g/1½ oz (1½ table-spoons) of the sugar, the egg, salt and grated lemon rind to the dough and knead until it comes away from the sides of the bowl. Cover and leave to rest for 20 minutes.

❸ Peel, quarter and core the apples. Cut the quarters into thin wedges. Grease a baking sheet with the softened margarine and roll out the well-kneaded dough on it. Sprinkle with the breadcrumbs. Arrange the apple wedges on the dough and sprinkle over the currants.

❹ Pre-heat oven to 200° C (400° F, Gas Mark 6).

❺ For the crumble: Mix the rest of the flour, sugar and vanilla sugar in a bowl. Melt the remaining butter, add to the dry ingredients and knead everything to a smooth dough. Rub into the crumble with your hands. Spread the crumble over the apple wedges and bake the cake for 30 to 40 minutes. Take from the oven and allow to cool.

Makes 12 pieces, 520 kcal per piece.

700 g/1½ lb (7 cups) lb plain (all purpose) flour

20 g/¾ oz yeast

250 g/8 oz (1 cup) sugar

125 ml/4 fl oz (½ cup) lukewarm milk

250 g/8 oz (1 cup) butter

1 egg

pinch of salt

peel from 1 unsprayed lemon

1 kg/2¼ lb cooking (green) apples

softened margarine

3 tablespoons breadcrumbs

100 g/3½ oz (⅔ cup) currants

1 sachet vanilla sugar

Rum and apple pie

This apple pie has a delicious apple and rum filling. You can also use raisins or currants. Simply add them to the apple mixture and bake as usual.

1 kg/2¼ lb apples

1 teaspoon sugar

1 teaspoon cinnamon

200 ml/7 fl oz (⅞ cup) rum

peel from 1 unsprayed lemon

375 g/12 oz (3½ cups) plain (all purpose) flour

250 g/8 oz (1 cup) butter

100 g/3½ oz (½ cup) sugar

60 g/2 oz (⅜ cup) grated almonds

4 eggs

softened margarine for the pie dish

icing (confectioners') sugar

❶ For the filling: Peel, quarter and core the apples. Cut the quarters into fine slices. Mix the sugar, cinnamon, rum and lemon peel in a bowl. Add the apple slices and marinate for 1 hour. Tip into a sieve and allow to drain well.

❷ For the dough: Sift the flour onto a board, make a hollow in the middle. Cut the butter into little pats and distribute around the edge. Put the sugar, almonds and 3 eggs into the hollow. Mix everything well and knead to a smooth dough. Wrap in a tea towel and refrigerate briefly.

❸ Take the dough out of the refrigerator and roll out to a thickness of 3 mm/⅛ in. Grease the pie dish with the margarine. Cut out two pieces of dough the same size as the dish. Put one in the bottom of the dish, pressing it firmly into the corners.

❹ Pre-heat the oven to 200°C (400°F), Gas Mark 6.

❺ Fill the dish with the apples. Cover with the second piece of dough and scallop the edges. Beat the remaining egg and brush the pie-crust with it. Put in the oven and bake for 45 minutes. Test with a skewer to see if it is done.

❻ Remove from the oven, cool on a wire rack and dust with icing (confectioners') sugar.

Makes 12 pieces, 500 kcal per piece.

Apple and wine cream pie

To be a success, this professional pie requires enough time for its preparation. In decorating it, there are no limits to the imagination. Try out all the various nozzles on your piping (decorators') bag and make it look as though it came from the patisserie.

❶ Peel, quarter and core the apples. Cut the quarters into thin wedges. Put the white wine into a saucepan with the sugar and cinnamon and bring briefly to the boil. Add the apple wedges and cook for 5 minutes. Drain, saving the liquid.

❷ For the wine cream: Put the egg yolks in a mixing bowl with the sugar, grated lemon peel and cornflour (cornstarch) and mix together. Add water to the apple cooking liquid to make it up to 500 ml/17 fl oz (2¼ cups). Add wine. Beat until foamy, bring briefly to the boil and leave to cool until lukewarm.

❸ Cover the sponge with the apple wedges. Add the lukewarm wine cream and spread smooth. Leave to cool completely.

❹ Melt the butter in a pan and roast the flaked (slivered) almonds until they are golden brown. Add the vanilla sugar to the cream and whip it until stiff.

❺ Put the whipped cream into a piping (decorators') bag and decorate the cake with it. Sprinkle with the roasted almonds.

Makes 12 pieces, 330 kcal per piece.

500 g/1 lb cooking (green) apples

250 ml/8 fl oz (1 cup) white wine

70 g/2½ oz (scant ⅓ cup) sugar

½ teaspoon cinnamon

For the cream:

4 egg yolks

125 g/4 oz (½ cup) sugar

peel from 1 unsprayed lemon

30 g/1 oz (3 tablespoons) cornflour (cornstarch)

125 ml/4 fl oz (½ cup) white wine

1 ready made sponge

2 tablespoons butter

100 g/3½ oz (scant 1 cup) flaked (slivered) almonds

375 ml/12 fl oz (1½ cups) cream

1 sachet vanilla sugar

Apple Chelsea pastries

These diminutive apple pastries are an exquisite delicacy. The dried apple rings and the pine kernels make them perfect for any occasion as well as a pleasant addition to a party buffet. Other nuts can be substituted in place of the rather expensive pine kernels if desired.

❶ Pre-heat oven to 180°C (350°F), Gas Mark 4.

❷ Cut the dried apple rings into little pieces and put in a bowl. Sprinkle with Calvados and leave to marinate for 30 minutes. Spread the pine kernels on a baking tray, put in the oven and roast until golden brown.

❸ Take the pine kernels out of the oven and allow to cool. Grind half of the kernels finely and chop the rest.

❹ Mix the flour and the cornflour (cornstarch) and sift into a bowl. Add the egg, sugar, soft butter or margarine, apple pieces and the ground pine kernels. Stir everything together and mix to a smooth dough, using a whisk. Put in the refrigerator to cool briefly.

❺ Take the dough out of the refrigerator and roll out to a rectangle about 30 x 35 cm (12 x14 in). Spread the apple jelly over it and sprinkle with the chopped pine kernels. Roll up carefully and return for a short time to the refrigerator.

❻ Turn the oven up to 200°C (400°F), Gas Mark 6.

❼ Take the roll out of the refrigerator and cut into slices 1 cm/½ in thick. Arrange the pieces on a baking sheet covered with parchment and bake for 20 to 25 minutes.

❽ Take the rolls out of the oven and leave to cool. Heat the apricot jam (jelly) in a small pan with 2 tablespoons of water and brush over the rolls.

Makes 12 pieces, 240 kcal per piece.

50 g/2 oz (⅓ cup) dried apple rings

3 tablespoons Calvados

100 g/3½ oz (1 cup) pine kernels

200 g/7 oz (2 cups) plain (all purpose) flour

50 g/2 oz (6 tablespoons) cornflour (cornstarch)

1 egg

50 g/2 oz (¼ cup) sugar

100 g/3½ oz (½ cup) softened margarine

2 tablespoons apple jelly

2 tablespoons apricot jam (jelly)

Apple turnovers

These homemade apple turnovers made from fresh apples are even nicer than the ready-made variety from the fast-food restaurants. The dough can be frozen in portions and thawed as needed to save time.

500 g/1 lb (4½ cups) plain (all purpose) flour

30 g/¾ oz (4 teaspoons) yeast

100 g/3½ oz (scant ½ cup) sugar

125 ml/4 fl oz (½ cup) lukewarm milk

100 g/3½ oz (scant ½ cup) softened butter

2 eggs

pinch of salt

500 g/1 lb cooking (green) apples

100 g/3½ oz (generous ½ cup) sultanas (golden raisins)

50 g/2 oz (⅓ cup) ground almonds

juice of 1 lemon

1 egg yolk

softened margarine for greasing the tray

❶ Put the flour into a mixing bowl and make a hollow in the middle. Crumble in the yeast. Add 20 g/¾ oz (¾ tablespoon) sugar and the lukewarm milk and stir to a smooth dough. Cover and leave to rest for 15 minutes.

❷ Cut the butter into small pieces and add to the dough along with 60 g/2 oz (1/4 cup) sugar, the eggs and the salt. Knead the dough until it comes away from the sides of the bowl. Cover and leave to rest for a further 20 minutes.

❸ Peel, quarter and core the apples. Dice finely and put in a bowl. Add the sultanas (golden raisins), almonds, the rest of the sugar and the lemon juice and stir.

❹ On a floured surface, roll out the pastry about ½ cm/³⁄₁₆ in thick and cut out rectangles roughly 12 x 14 cm/5 x 5½ in in size. Place spoonfuls of the filling in the middle of the rectangles. Whisk the egg yolk and brush along the edges of the pastry. Fold over to make triangles and press the edges together.

❺ Pre-heat oven to 200°C (400°F), Gas Mark 6.

❻ Brush the turnovers with the remaining egg yolk. Grease a baking sheet with the margarine and leave the turnovers to rest for a further 10 minutes before putting in the oven on the middle shelf and baking for 20 minutes. Test with a skewer to see if they are done. Remove from the oven and leave to cool on a wire rack.

Makes 12 turnovers, 340 kcal each.

Apple fritters

These are sweet apple rings cooked in batter. Apple fritters taste wonderful when served with coffee. They can also be served with a glass of dry white wine or prosecco, or with a warming mug of mulled wine in the winter. For the winter variation, add some cinnamon to the sugar.

650 g/1½ lb apples

2 tablespoons sugar

2 eggs

125 g/4 oz (1¼ cups) plain (all purpose) flour

2 tablespoons milk

2 tablespoons oil

pinch of salt

fat for deep-frying

❶ Peel the apples and remove the cores carefully. Cut the apples into thick rings. Sprinkle with sugar and set aside.

❷ Separate the eggs. Put flour, milk, egg yolk, oil and salt in a mixing bowl and mix to a smooth batter. Beat the egg whites until they are stiff and fold carefully into the batter.

❸ Heat the fat in a large saucepan.

❹ Dip the apple rings into the batter, turn them over to cover them completely and slip immediately into the hot fat . Cook to a golden brown.

❺ Remove the fritters from the fat, drain on a kitchen towel and sprinkle with sugar.

Makes 12 fritters, 130 kcal each.

Apple sponge slices

These sponge slices are light and delicious. This black and white version is particularly digestible since it contains very little fat.

❶ Separate the eggs. In a bowl, whisk the egg yolks with two-thirds of the sugar. Beat the egg whites with the rest of the sugar until stiff. Add to the egg yolks and fold in carefully. Sift the flour and the baking powder and add to the eggs. Stir in carefully.

❷ Peel the apples and remove the cores. Cut into rings. Grease a baking tray and sprinkle with the breadcrumbs. Lay a layer of apple rings on the tray and pour over half the sponge batter.

❸ Pre-heat oven to 150 C (300°F), Gas Mark 2.

❹ Sift the cocoa over the second half of the batter, stir in and mix well. Pour over the light batter.

❺ Bake in the pre-heated oven for about one hour. Test with a skewer to see if it is done.

❻ Remove the cake from the oven and leave to cool. Remove from the tray and cut into 12 pieces. Sprinkle with icing (confectioners') sugar.

Makes 12 pieces, 210 kcal per piece.

4 eggs

200 g/7 oz (scant 1 cup) sugar

200 g/7 oz (2 cups) plain (all purpose) flour

½ sachet baking powder

800 g/1¾ lb apples

margarine for the baking tray

breadcrumbs for the baking tray

20 g/¾ oz (scant ¼ cup) cocoa

icing (confectioners') sugar

Desserts

Fruity, light desserts are becoming more and more popular in today's cuisine. Apples are always perfect for rounding off a meal, whether combined with strawberries (Apple and strawberry tartlets, page 109), ice cream (Apple and vanilla ice cream, page 110), with curd (farmer's) cheese (Apple and curd cheese casserole, page 127), or as a casserole or flambé. They are healthy, and their high content of fructose and glucose makes them good suppliers of energy.

Beignets à la Princesse

Beignets are a richer version of the humble fritter. Serve them with a compote or with fresh fruit. The batter can also be used for preparing other fruits . Try using pineapple, bananas and strawberries to make a colourful beignet potpourri.

1.3 kg/2½ lb apples

2 teaspoons sugar

2 tablespoons rum

peel from ½ unsprayed lemon

125 g/4 oz (1¼ cups) plain (all purpose) flour

2 eggs

pinch of salt

1 tablespoon oil

fat for deep-frying

1 packet custard

❶ Peel the apples and core them. Cut into thick slices and put in a bowl. Add sugar, 1 tablespoon of rum and the lemon peel and stir carefully.

❷ Separate the eggs. Put flour, egg yolks and 200 ml/7 fl oz (⅞ cup) water into a bowl and stir to a thick batter.

❸ Add salt, oil and the rest of the rum to the batter and mix. Beat the egg whites until they form peaks and fold into the batter.

❹ Heat the fat in a deep pan. Dip the slices of apple into the batter and deep-fry to a golden brown. Remove the apple rings from the fat and drain on kitchen paper.

❺ Make the custard according to the instructions on the packet and serve with the beignets.

Serves four, 530 kcal per serving.

Ginger apples flambé

This is a fiery dessert in more ways than one and it is quite an attraction when flambéed at the table in front of your guests. Serve with either whipped cream or vanilla ice cream.

500 g/1 lb untreated apples

2 teaspoons lemon juice

softened butter for the dish

4 tablespoons sugar

2 pieces of ginger in syrup

2 tablespoons sultanas (golden raisins)

4 small glasses of brandy

❶ Wash the apples thoroughly. Remove the cores without cutting up the apples and slice off the top of each one.

❷ Brush the lemon juice on the inside of the apples. Grease an oven-proof dish with butter. Put the apples in it and sprinkle with sugar.

❸ Pre-heat oven to 200°C (400°F), Gas Mark 6.

❹ Dice the ginger very finely and mix with the sultanas (golden raisins). Fill the apples with the mixture. Bake in the oven for 15 minutes on the middle shelf.

❺ Take the apples out of the oven, pour the brandy over and set alight.

Serves four, 180 kcal per serving.

Baked apples in pastry

For this recipe you ready-prepared pastry can be used, since making a yeast dough is quite time-consuming. Practised cooks can, of course, make their own.

❶ Make the pastry according to the instructions.

❷ Sift the flour onto the work surface and roll the dough out on it. Cut out 4 square and 4 circular pieces of dough.

❸ Wash the apples thoroughly. Carefully remove the cores. Knead the raw marzipan with the orange juice and the almonds. Season with cinnamon and fill the apples with the mixture.

❹ Pre-heat oven to 200°C (400°F), Gas Mark 6.

❺ Set an apple in the middle of each square of dough. Fold up the corners to cover the apple and put the round piece on top to cover. Brush everything with the egg yolk.

❻ Grease the baking tray with the softened margarine and arrange the apples on it. Bake for 20 to 25 minutes. Remove from the oven and leave to cool on a wire rack.

Serves four, 360 kcal per serving.

1 packet yeast pastry

flour for the work surface

500 g/1 lb untreated apples

60 g/2 oz (4 tablespoons) marzipan

4 tablespoons orange juice

3 tablespoons chopped almonds

1 teaspoon cinnamon

1 egg yolk

softened margarine for the baking tray

Apple and strawberry tartlets

These small pastries are fresh and fruity. You can buy the little pie cases ready-made. With the sweet apple topping they are a delicious dessert.

❶ Peel the apples, cut in half and remove the cores. Put the apple halves in a bowl and sprinkle with lemon juice.

❷ Put 250 ml/8 fl oz (1 cup) water and the white wine in a saucepan and bring to the boil. Add the sugar and the apple halves and cook for about 10 minutes. Take the apples out of the liquor and drain. Allow to cool.

❸ Melt the chocolate coating in a pan set over boiling water. Brush the inside of the tart cases with the melted coating and set aside to cool.

❹ Put the apples in the pastry cases with the core side down, brush with strawberry jam (jelly) and decorate with the almonds.

❺ Wash the strawberries and remove the stalk ends. Make a crosswise cut from the pointed end and pull the quarters slightly apart. Put on top of the apple halves. Whip the cream and put 1 spoonful in each of the open strawberries. Sprinkle with the pistachios.

Serves four, 530 kcal per serving.

250 g/8 oz apples

juice of ½ lemon

250 ml/8 fl oz (1 cup) white wine

2 tablespoons sugar

4 tartlet cases

80 g/3 oz (⅜ cup) chocolate coating

4 teaspoons strawberry jam (jelly)

50 g/2 oz (½ cup) flaked (slivered) almonds

4 strawberries

125 ml/4 fl oz (½ cup) cream

1 tablespoon chopped pistachios

Apple and vanilla ice cream

These apples with chocolate icing make a magical dessert. It is easy to make using ready-made ice cream. The sauce is also quickly made using condensed milk.

500 g/1 lb apples

4 scoops of vanilla ice cream

40 g/1½ oz (⅜ cup) cocoa

50 g/2 oz (¼ cup) sugar

125 ml/4 fl oz (½ cup) condensed milk

1 teaspoon cornflour (cornstarch)

❶ Peel the apples, cut in half and remove the cores and. Put the apples in a saucepan with some water and cook briefly. Set aside.

❷ In a small saucepan, stir the cocoa and sugar into the condensed milk and bring to the boil. Remove the pan from the heat and thicken the sauce with the cornflour (cornstarch). Set aside to cool in the refrigerator.

❸ Put the apples with the core side uppermost in four small bowls. Fill each apple half with a scoop of ice cream.

❹ Take the chocolate sauce out of the refrigerator and pour over the vanilla ice cream. Serve immediately.

Serves four, 260 kcal per serving.

Apple and walnut parfait

An ice cream parlour is not the only place to find ice cream. You can also make it at home. This recipe with apples and walnuts is easy to make yourself and still tastes as though you were on the Riviera.

❶ Peel, quarter and core the apples. Cut into small dice and put in a saucepan. Keep some for garnishing later. Add 200 ml/7 fl oz (⅞ cup) water, 1 tablespoon sugar and the cinnamon stick and cook everything for 10 minutes. Drain well.

❷ Put 125 ml/4 fl oz (½ cup) water into a small saucepan with the remaining sugar and cook for 5 minutes until it thickens. Remove from heat and leave to cool. Add the egg yolk to the cooled syrup and stir until creamy. Stand the pan in a larger sucepan of boiling water and whisk until it foams. Remove from heat and keep whisking until it cools.

❸ Whip the cream and fold into the syrup. Keep aside some walnuts for decoration and finely chop the remainder. Stir the chopped walnuts and the diced apple into the syrup and put in the freezer for about three hours.

❹ Fill four glasses with the parfait and serve garnished with some apple cubes and walnut halves.

Serves four, 470 kcal per serving.

400 g/14 oz apples
100 g/3½ oz (½ cup) ugar
½ stick of cinnamon
3 egg yolks
250 ml/8 fl oz (1 cup) cream
75 g/3 oz (¾ cup) walnuts

Glace aux pommes

This exquisite French apple sherbet is made without milk and is therefore very easy to digest. It is also suitable for those who suffer from lactose intolerance.

❶ Peel, quarter and core the apples. Set aside some quarters for the decoration and grate the rest. Put in a bowl and add the brown sugar. Mix well.

❷ Dissolve the white sugar in some water. Add 500 ml/17 fl oz (2¼ cups) water and the lemon juice. Mix together with the apple mixture.

❸ Drain the apple mixture well through a fine sieve, then put the dry apple mixture in a bowl and put it in the freezer.

❹ Scoop out spoonfuls of the ice-sherbet and serve in glass bowls garnished with thin apple slices.

Serves four, 315 kcal per serving.

500 g/1 lb apples

90 g/3 oz (⅜ cup) demerara (light brown) sugar

140 g/5 oz (¾ cup) white sugar

juice of ½ lemon

Apples with custard

This simple dessert is very popular with children. They can even help make it, arranging the prepared ingredients in the bowl.

650 g/1½ lb apples
50 g/2 oz (¼ cup) sugar
1 packet custard
8 sponge fingers
whipped cream to taste

❶ Peel and cut the apples in half. Remove the cores. Dissolve the sugar in a saucepan with some water and add the apples. Cook until soft, but do not let the apples become too mushy.

❷ Make the custard following the instructions on the packet.

❸ Put the sponge fingers in a glass bowl. Arrange the apple halves on top. Spoon the custard onto the apples. Decorate as desired with whipped cream.

Serves four, 270 kcal per serving.

Chilled apple soup

This is an old recipe from France in which the apples are cooked in wine and served chilled. It can be served with ice cream or whipped cream.

500 g/1 lb apples
200 ml/7 fl oz (⅞ cup) white wine
180 g/6 oz (¾ cup) sugar
juice of 1 lemon
40 g/1½ oz (¼ cup) sultanas
  (golden raisins)
40 g/1½ oz (¼ cup) currants

❶ Peel, quarter and core the apples. Cut one-third of them into fine slices and put in a shallow casserole. Pour over 40 ml/2 fl oz (4 table-spoons) of white wine, 60 g/2 oz (¼ cup) sugar and 1 tablespoon of lemon juice. Cook over a medium heat until the apples are soft.

❷ Cut the remaining apples into fine slices and put in a large saucepan. Add one-third of the lemon juice and 100 ml/3½ fl oz (scant ½ cup) water. Cook until soft. Line a sieve with kitchen towel, pour in the apple mixture and let it drain well.

❸ Put the drained apple sauce in a bowl and mix with 120 g/4 oz (½ cup) sugar, the rest of the lemon juice and 160 ml/5½ fl oz (¾ cup) white wine. Spoon over the apples in the casserole.

❹ Pour boiling water over the sultanas (golden raisins) and the currants and drain well. Sprinkle over the apples.

Serves four, 350 kcal per serving.

Apple temptation with candied flower petals

This is pure temptation – apples in zabaglione. It is a dessert to be kept for special occasions. The candied flower petals and the white wine zabaglione make it the perfect dessert to complete a romantic dinner for two.

❶ Peel the apples, cut in half and remove the cores. Bring a saucepan of water to the boil and cook the apples until soft.

❷ Remove the apple halves from the water and put into four small bowls, core side down. Sprinkle with the chopped almonds.

❸ Pour the apple juice into a saucepan with the salt and the sugar and bring to the boil. Stir some water into the cornflour (cornstarch) and use it to thicken the apple juice. Remove the pan from the heat and stir the egg yolk carefully into the thickened apple juice. Gradually add the white wine .

❹ Beat the egg whites until they form peaks and fold lightly and carefully into the apple juice mixture. Spread the zabaglione around the apples and garnish with the violets or rose petals.

Serves four, 220 kcal per serving.

500 g/1 lb apples

30 g/1 oz (¼ cup) chopped almonds

125 ml/4 fl oz (½ cup) apple juice

pinch of salt

2 teaspoons sugar

1 tablespoon cornflour (cornstarch)

1 egg yolk

250 ml/8 fl oz (1 cup) white wine

some candied violets or rose petals

Apple confection

This is a sweet delicacy for a loved one, perhaps served as a dessert after a special candlelight dinner. It also makes a nice gift when presented in a pretty box.

200 g/7 oz apples

150 g/5 oz (⅔ cup) sugar

30 g/1 oz (2 tablespoons) candied lemon peel

100 g/3½ oz (¾ cup) chopped almonds

juice of 1 lemon

50 g/2 oz (5 tablespoons) light-coloured jam (jelly)

small rice wafers.

❶ Peel, quarter and core the apples. Cut the quarters into small pieces.

❷ Heat 125 ml/4 fl oz (½ cup) water in a saucepan. Add the sugar and the apples. Cook until they are on the point of disintegrating.

❸ Cut up the lemon peel and mix into the apple sauce together with the chopped almonds, the lemon juice and the jam (jelly).

❹ Pre-heat the oven to 150°C (300°F), Gas Mark 2.

❺ Scoop out small amounts of the mixture with a teaspoon and drop onto the wafers. Line a baking tray with greaseproof paper, put the wafers on it and allow to dry in the warm oven.

❻ Remove the wafers from the oven and cool on a wire rack.

Serves four, 380 kcal per serving.

Apple surprise

A pleasant surprise for children of all ages. This dessert looks like a custard, but there is a secret inside: an apple filled with jam (jelly). This is a treat for young and old.

4 large apples

1 tablespoon sugar

8 tablespoons jam (jelly)

1 packet red jelly (jello)

1 packet custard

❶ Peel the apples and core them carefully.

❷ Dissolve the sugar in a pan of water. Add the apples. Put on the heat and cook the apples until soft.

❸ Remove the apples from the water and fill with the jam (jelly). Put each apple in a pudding bowl.

❹ Make the jelly (jello) according to the instructions on the packet and set aside to cool. Pour over the apples and refrigerate.

❺ Take the apples out of the refrigerator. Make the custard according to the instructions, pour over the jelly and smooth with a spatula. Return to the refrigerator.

❻ Once the pudding has cooled properly, remove from refrigerator and turn upside down on a plate.

Serves four, 240 kcal per serving.

Apple magic

You can create magic with this wonderful dessert of custard and apples. It can be served on festive occasions, or, if you leave out the custard and the sponge fingers, you can serve the filled apples as a side dish to game or poultry.

4 apples

juice of 1 lemon

50 g/2 oz (¼ cup) sugar

100 g/3½ oz sponge fingers

150 g/5 oz (scant ½ cup) cranberry preserve

50 g/2 oz (½ cup) chopped almonds

250 ml/8 fl oz (1 cup) milk

½ packet custard

20 g/¾ oz butter

2 egg yolks

20 g/¾ oz (⅛ cup) fresh cranberries

❶ Peel the apples and remove the cores carefully. Put them in a casserole and sprinkle with lemon juice and 4 tablespoons of sugar. Add 125 ml/4 fl oz (½ cup) water and cook the apples.

❷ Remove the apples from the heat and put on a plate. Crumble the sponge fingers and put them in a bowl. Add the cranberry preserve and almonds and mix. Fill the apples with this mixture.

❸ Stir the milk, custard powder, remaining sugar, butter and egg yolks in a bowl over a pan of hot water until the mixture is a smooth, creamy consistency. Set aside to cool.

❹ Wash and pick over the cranberries. Once the cream has cooled, pour over the apples and garnish with the cranberries.

Serves four, 500 kcal per serving.

Apple sauce

You can serve apple sauce as a dessert if you add cream. It is very good with sweet dishes such as pancakes (crepes), sweet omelettes or sweet yeast dumplings cooked in milk. It can also be serve as a side dish to substantial meals such as potato pancakes (crepes) or pork.

1 kg/2¼ lb untreated apples

peel from ½ unsprayed lemon

100 g/3½ oz (½ cup) sugar

raisins or currants for garnishing

❶ Wash the apples thoroughly, cut into eighths and remove the cores.

❷ Heat 125 ml/4 fl oz (½ cup) water in a saucepan, add the pieces of apple and the lemon peel. Cook until soft, stirring all the while.

❸ Press the apple and lemon mixture through a sieve and put back into the pan. Cook to a thick sauce. Remove from heat and allow to cool.

❹ Fill small glass bowls with the apple sauce and garnish with raisins or currants.

Serves four, 250 kcal per serving.

Apple preserve

This apple compote keeps well because of the vinegar. You can put it up in jars and you will always have something on hand to make into a quick meal. For maximum speed, use it with ready-made pancakes (crepes) which only need heating in the pan. Open a jar of this apple preserve to go with them, and there is your lunch!

❶ Peel, quarter and core the apples. Cut the quarters into small pieces.

❷ Heat 125 ml/4 fl oz (½ cup) water in a saucepan. Add the apples, vinegar and sugar and stew to a compote while stirring constantly.

❸ Remove the pan from the heat and pour the preserve into jars. Do not put the lids on yet.

❹ Allow the preserve to cool in the jars. Cut the parchment to size, dip it in the rum and lay on top of the compote. Screw the lids on tightly.

Serves four, 660 kcal per serving.

1 kg/2¼ lb apples
500 g/1 lb (2½ cups) sugar
4 tablespoons vinegar
1 tablespoon rum
parchment paper

Fresh apple compote

This recipe has been handed down from many years ago. It can be made in two ways. It tastes best when eaten fresh and still warm – with pancakes (crepes) or blinis, for instance. A large dollop of ice cream is also a good accompaniment.

Variation 1:
750 g/1½ lb apples
peel from ½ untreated lemon
1 teaspoon cinnamon
70 g/2½ oz (scant ⅓ cup) sugar

Variation 1:

❶ Peel, quarter and core apples. Cut the quarters into small pieces.

❷ Heat 125 ml/4 fl oz (½ cup) water in a pan. Add the pieces of apple, lemon peel, cinnamon and sugar. Cook everything on a low heat until soft. Sweeten to taste.

Variation 2:
750 g/1½ lb apples
juice of 1 lemon
1 teaspoon cinnamon
70 g/2½ oz (scant ⅓ cup) sugar

Variation 2:

❶ Peel, quarter and core the apples. Cut the quarters into small pieces.

❷ Put sugar and 125 ml/4 fl oz (½ cup) water in a pan and bring to the boil. Add the pieces of apple and the lemon juice and simmer until thick. Sweeten to taste.

Serves four, 180 kcal per serving.

Raspberry apple compote

This is a modern apple compote. The addition of raspberries turns this simple dish into an especially delicious delight for the discriminating palate.

❶ Wash the raspberries and put in a bowl. Sprinkle the fruit with icing (confectioners') sugar and refrigerate.

❷ Peel, quarter and core the apples. Cut one third into fine slices and the remainder into small pieces.

❸ Put the apple slices into a pan and sprinkle with 80 g/3 oz (generous 1/3 cup) of the sugar. Add lemon juice and 1 tablespoon of water and cook for 3 minutes. Remove pan from the heat and leave the apple slices to cool.

❹ Cook the small pieces of apple in 375 ml/12 fl oz (1½ cups) water and the rest of the sugar until soft.

❺ Press the apple sauce through a sieve. Add the apple slices, raspberries and white wine. Refrigerate. Serve cold with sponge fingers.

Serves four, 550 kcal per serving.

100 g/3½ oz (⅔ cup) raspberries

50 g/2 oz (scant ½ cup) icing (confectioners') sugar

500 g/1 lb cooking (green) apples

280 g/10 oz (1⅓ cups) sugar

2 tablespoons lemon juice

750 ml/1¼ pints (3¼ cups) white wine

several sponge fingers

Tipsy apple and peach salad

It is the marzipan, honey and herb liqueur which distinguish this special fruit salad. Made with a herb liqueur which is a pure essences of herbs, your dessert will be healthy as well as delicious.

❶ Peel, quarter and core the apples. Cut into slices and put in a bowl. Sprinkle immediately with lemon juice and mix.

❷ Wash the peaches, stone and cut into thin wedges. Add to the apples in the bowl and mix carefully.

❸ Mix the marzipan with the honey, liqueur and cream. Stir into the fruit and fill small bowls with the salad. Chop the walnuts and sprinkle over the salad before serving.

Serves four, 430 kcal per serving.

550 g/1¼ lb untreated apples

juice of 1 lemon

3 peaches

50 g/2 oz (4 tablespoons) marzipan

1 tablespoon honey

6 tablespoons herb liqueur

6 tablespoons cream

100 g/3½ oz (1 cup) walnuts

Apple rings with vanilla cream

This is a lightning fast dessert when you are in a hurry. It is also a light dish that is permissible even when one is keeping an eye on one's weight.

800 g/1½ lb untreated apples

375 ml/12 fl oz (1½ cups) dry white wine

3 tablespoons sugar

juice of 1 lemon

1 teaspoon cinnamon

pinch of grated nutmeg

125 ml/4 fl oz (½ cup) cream

1 sachet vanilla sugar

❶ Wash the apples thoroughly. Remove the cores carefully and cut the apples into slices 1 cm/½ in thick.

❷ Mix the white wine, sugar, lemon juice, cinnamon and nutmeg in a saucepan. Add the apples and bring briefly to the boil. Simmer over a low heat for about 5 minutes. Remove the apple rings from the pan and drain on a kitchen towel. Refrigerate for 30 minutes.

❸ Whip the cream. Fold in the vanilla sugar carefully. Take the apple rings out of the refrigerator and serve with the cream.

Serves four, 290 kcal per serving.

Apple and curd (farmer's) cheese casserole

This casserole makes a very rich dessert. It would be best to serve it after a very light main course. It can also be served as a main course itself, in which case, a light fruit salad would be suitable as a dessert.

❶ Put the lemon juice, 20 g/¾ oz (¾ tablepoon) of the sugar, cinnamon and cardamom in a bowl and mix. Peel, quarter and core the apples. Cut the quarters into thin slices and mix into the lemon juice mixture immediately. Set aside to marinate for 20 minutes.

❷ Separate the eggs. Stir the curd (farmer's) cheese, the egg yolks and the rest of the sugar to a smooth paste. Mix the baking powder with the semolina and fold carefully into the cheese mixture.

❸ Add the marinated apples to the batter. Beat the egg whites until they form peaks and add to the mixture.

❹ Pre-heat the oven to 200°C (400°F), Gas Mark 6.

❺ Grease an ovenproof dish with the margarine and sprinkle with the breadcrumbs. Pour in the cheese mixture. Bake on the bottom shelf of the oven. If it becomes too brown, cover with foil.

Serves four, 470 kcal per serving.

juice of 1 lemon

120 g/4 oz (generous ½ cup) sugar

½ teaspoon cinnamon

pinch of cardamom

500 g/1 lb apples

500 g/1 lb curd (farmer's) cheese

3 eggs

60 g/2 oz (1/3 cup) semolina

2 tablespoons baking powder

softened margarine for the dish

2 tablespoons breadcrumbs

Baked apples

Baked apples are redolent of winter evenings and Christmas. In this recipe, they are given little snowy caps of meringue. Serve them with custard or whipped cream for a delicious winter treat.

550 g/1¼ lb untreated apples

2 tablespoons butter

3 tablespoons caraway schnapps (such as Kümmel)

3 tablespoons sugar

1 egg white

sprinkling of cinnamon

8 tablespoons apple sauce

2 tablespoons chopped almonds

❶ Wash the apples thoroughly and cut a little 'lid' off the top of each one. Carefully remove the cores from the whole apples and hollow out a little. Mix the butter with 2 tablespoons of the caraway schnapps and 2 tablespoons of sugar and spoon into the apples.

❷ Pre-heat oven to 225°C (435°F), Gas Mark 7.

❸ Grease an oven dish with the remaining butter. Arrange the apples in it and bake for 25 minutes.

❹ Beat the egg white with the remaining sugar and the cinnamon until it forms peaks. Mix the apple sauce with the remainder of the caraway schnapps. Take the apples out of the oven. Fill with the apple sauce and spoon on the beaten egg whites.

❺ Return to the oven on the top shelf and bake until golden yellow.

Serves four, 250 kcal per serving.

Beverages and sauces

Apples can also be made into excellent sauces and beverages, with or without alcohol. They are wonderful for making unfiltered or clear juice, and for drinks such as the health-promoting Apple-peel tea (page 132) and the Apple vinegar drink (page 135). Apples also add an extra dimension to mayonnaise (page 151) and cream (page 150), while home-made apple jam (jelly) (page 143) is absolutely delicious.

Apple-peel tea

It is very easy to make your own apple-peel tea. It can be enjoy on its own or mixed with other kinds, such as green tea or rooibos tea.

200 g/7 oz apple peel
sugar or honey to taste
1 untreated apple

❶ Wash the apple peels thoroughly, spread out on a large cloth and leave to dry for several days.

❷ Put 1 litre/1¾ pints (4½ cups) cold water in a saucepan, add the apple-peel and boil for 10 minutes. Pour through a sieve into a jug.

❸ Wash the apple thoroughly and peel it so that the peel comes off in a long spiral. Add sugar or honey to the tea and use some of the spiral apple peel as a garnish.

Makes 1 litre/13/4 pints (41/2 cups), 10 kcal per cup.

Apple juice

You can make apple juice yourself if you know how. It is a rather time-consuming process but well worth it, since you are in charge of what goes into the juice.

2.5 kg/5 lb sour, untreated apples

500 g sugar per litre of apple juice, or 1 lb sugar per 1½ pints (4 cups) of apple juice

❶ Wash the apples thoroughly, remove the cores and quarter.

❷ Cook the apples in 2½ litres/4½ pints (11 cups) of water until soft. Line a sieve with cheesecloth, pour in the cooked apples and allow to drain. Leave to stand overnight.

❸ Add the sugar to the apple juice. Put in a large pan, bring to the boil and cook for 15 minutes.

❹ Remove the pan from the stove and set aside to cool. Pour through a funnel into sterilized bottles and seal with airtight tops.

Makes 1 litre/1¾ pints (4½ cups), 130 kcal per glass.

Apple water

This is a variation of the recipe for apple juice. A wonderfully refreshing drink on a hot summer's day, it is also a healthy alternative to lemonade. If honey is used instead of sugar, the drink makes an ideal accompaniment for a meal.

1 Wash the apples thoroughly, cut into eighths and remove the cores.

2 Bring 1 ½ litres water to the boil in a large saucepan. Add cinnamon, lemon peel and apples and cook for about 15 minutes until the apples are soft. Line a sieve with cheesecloth, tip in the apples and drain into a jug.

3 Sweeten the apple water with sugar or honey and leave to cool. Serve chilled.

Makes 1 litre/1¾ pints (4½ cups), 10 kcal per glass.

1.5 kg/3 lb untreated apples
cinnamon
peel from 1 unsprayed lemon
sugar or honey

Apple vinegar drink

There are great healing powers in apple vinegar as it helps the body's self-purification system. It is also a wonderful marinade for fish, meat or poultry. The fruity-sour taste enhances the flavour of any kind of salad or raw food.

1 Mix the apple vinegar with the buckthorn juice and the honey.

2 Add the mineral water and serve chilled.

Makes 1 litre/1¾ pints (4½ cups), 10 kcal per glass.

2 tablespoons apple vinegar
1 tablespoon buckthorn juice
1 teaspoon honey
1 litre/1¾ pints (4½ cups) mineral water

Apple and bilberry (blueberry) drink

Bilberries (blueberries) are full of goodness. They used to be one of the most important sources of food for the American Indians, and were thought to protect against evil spirits. The dark purplish-blue berries can sometimes be found growing in the woods in the summer and can be picked for your drink. Otherwise, frozen ones can be used all the year round.

500 g/1 lb untreated apples

2 tablespoons bilberries (blueberries)

1 unsprayed lemon

juice of ½ lemon

❶ Wash the apples thoroughly and cut into quarters. Wash and pick over the bilberries (blueberries).

❷ Juice the apples and the bilberries (blueberries) in a juicer, add lemon juice to taste and pour into glasses.

❸ Wash the lemon well and cut into eighths. Put a wedge of lemon on the edge of each glass.

Makes 1 litre/1¾ pints (4½ cups), 10 kcal per glass.

Apple-beer punch

The apple water with spices and lemon juice harmonises wonderfully with the beer in this recipe. This is a special drink, ideal for summer barbecues and garden parties.

500 g/1 lb apples
juice of 1 lemon
150 g/5 oz (⅔ cup) sugar
2 cloves
cinnamon
1 untreated lemon
600 ml/1 pint (2½ cups) beer

❶ Peel, quarter and core the apples. Cut the quarters into thin slices.

❷ Stir the sugar, cloves and cinnamon into the lemon juice. Put in a pan with the apple slices and bring briefly to the boil. Take the pan off the stove and set aside to cool.

❸ Wash the lemon thoroughly and cut into slices. Mix the cooled apple mixture with the beer and lemon slices and serve ice cold.

Makes 1 litre/1¾ pints (4½ cups), 280 kcal per glass.

Apple-woodruff punch

This apple punch is a particularly sparkling treat for summer parties, large and small. It is also a good drink for a dazzling New Year's Eve. The combination of wine and champagne is very stimulating as long as one does not drink too much.

Remember to start preparations well in advance.

❶ Peel, quarter and core the apples. Cut into fine slices and put in a bowl. Pour 750 ml/1¼ pints (3¼ cups) of wine over them immediately to stop them turning brown.

❷ Dissolve the sugar in a glass of wine and pour over the apples. Add the cinnamon and lemon peel and leave everything to steep for at least 10 hours.

❸ Add the champagne or sparkling wine and the rest of the white wine and refrigerate. Wash the woodruff and pinch off the leaves. Garnish the punch with the leaves before serving.

Makes 3 litres, 200 kcal per glass.

1 kg/2 lb apples

1.5 litres/2¾ pints (4½ cups) white wine

2 teaspoons sugar

1 stick of cinnamon

peel from 1 unsprayed lemon

1 sprig woodruff

1 bottle of champagne or sparkling wine

Apple milkshake

Apples and milk – a power drink for anyone whose need for vitamins and protein is high. It is particularly recommended for athletes who need an extra helping of energy before training sessions.

1 kg/2¼ lb untreated apples
1 litre/1¾ pints (4½ cups) milk
4 egg yolks
8 tablespoons honey

❶ Wash the apples thoroughly, remove the cores and quarter. Cut one of the quarters into thin slices and set aside for the decoration.

❷ Put the milk in a blender. Add the apple quarters, egg yolks and honey. Blend thoroughly.

❸ Pour the apple milkshake into tall glasses and garnish with the reserved apple slices.

Makes 1 litre/1¾ pints (4½ cups), 480 kcal per glass.

Elderberry and apple jam (jelly)

Home-made jams (jellies) are a special treat today. This elderberry and apple variation is a welcome change from the kinds more commonly offered. It makes breakfast into a special event.

❶ Wash and pick over the elderberries, then drain very well. Pluck the berries carefully from the stalks, weigh out 600 g/1¼ lb and set aside.

❷ Peel, quarter and core the apples. Cut 5 apples into small pieces. Cut a further apple into small pieces and reserve.

❸ Put the elderberries into a large saucepan with the pieces of apple. Add the lemon peel, lemon juice, ginger and preserving sugar. Bring to the boil while stirring and boil for 4 minutes.

❹ Remove the pan from the heat, add the remaining elderberries and apples and pour the still hot jam (jelly) into clean jars. Break the stick of cinnamon into small pieces. Push a piece into each jar. Close the jars, making them airtight and store in a cool place. Once opended, use within a week.

Makes 1.5 kg/3 lb jam (jelly), 55 kcal per serving.

800 g/1¾ lb (cups) elderberries

800 g/1¾ lb apples

peel and juice of 1 unsprayed lemon

½ teaspoon ground ginger

1 kg/2¼ lb (5 cups) preserving sugar

1 stick of cinnamon

Special apple jam (jelly)

This special jam (jelly) will not just sweeten your breakfast; as a little gift it will keep a friendship sweet, too. A prettily wrapped jar of apple jam (jelly) makes a delightful present to give to friends.

1 kg/2¼ lb cooking (green) apples

2 tablespoons vinegar

peel and juice of 1 unsprayed lemon

1 kg/2¼ lb (5 cups) sugar

½ bottle pectin

❶ Peel, quarter and core the apples. Keep the apple peel and the cores. Put some water and the vinegar in a bowl and add the apple quarters.

❷ Heat a saucepan with 250 ml/8 fl oz (1 cup) water. Add the peel and the cores and boil for 20 minutes till soft. Remove from heat and press through a sieve to make an apple purée.

❸ Measure 250 ml/8 fl oz (1 cup) of the apple purée and put in a pan with the lemon peel, lemon juice and sugar, mixing well. Bring the purée to the boil. Remove the apple quarters from the vinegar and water and dice. Add the diced apple quarters to the apple purée and cook until they are soft but still hold their shape.

❹ Stir in the pectin, bring briefly to the boil and remove the pan from the heat. Pour the jam (jelly) into jars while it is still hot and seal tightly. Store in a cool place. After opening, use within a week.

Makes 1.5 kg, 60 kcal per serving.

Apple relish

Relishes, like chutneys, are spicy and appetizing condiments that go with nearly all meat and poultry dishes. This relish can also be used as an ingredient for special dishes, for instance, as a spice for sauces or in a pasta salad. Remember to start the day before.

❶ Peel the onion and chop coarsely. Chop the sultanas (golden raisins). Peel and chop the ginger. Peel the garlic and crush with some salt.

❷ Peel, quarter and core the apples. Cut the quarters into very small pieces. Mix with the onions, sultanas (golden raisins), ginger, garlic, lemon peel and lemon juice. Pour everything into a stoneware bowl.

❸ Put the wine vinegar into a saucepan with 125 ml/4 fl oz (½ cup) water and the sugar and mix well. Add the chilli pepper and the cloves. Bring quickly to the boil and continue boiling for 4 minutes. Take the pan from the stove and pour the contents over the apple mixture. Cover and leave to stand for 12 hours.

❹ Pour the apple mixture into a preserving pan or large saucepan and simmer for 3 hours over a low heat until it thickens. Stir occasionally. After cooking for one hour, remove the chilli pepper and the cloves.

❺ Remove the pan from the heat and season further if desired. Pour into clean jars and seal tightly. After opening keep in the refrigerator and use within one week.

Serves four, 440 kcal per serving.

300 g/10 oz onions

250 g/8 oz (1⅓ cups) sultanas (golden raisins)

75 g/3 oz fresh ginger

2 cloves of garlic

2 teaspoons salt

125 g/4 oz apples

peel and juice of ½ lemon

750 ml/1¼ pints (3¼ cups) white wine vinegar

200 g/7 oz (1 cup) brown sugar

3 small dried chilli peppers

3 cloves

Apple chutney

This chutney can be stored like a preserve. The sweet-and-sour flavour goes well with all meat and poultry dishes. It is also perfect as an accompaniment to Asian rice dishes.

1 kg/2¼ lb firm apples
1 large onion
150 g/5 oz (scant 1 cup) raisins
1 tablespoon mustard seed
1 teaspoon salt
pinch of pepper
600 g/1¼ lb (3 cups) coarse sugar
250 ml/8 fl oz (1 cup) wine
  vinegar

❶ Peel, quarter and core apples. Cut the quarters into fine slices.

❷ Peel the onion and cut small.

❸ Mix the onions and apples with the raisins, mustard seed, salt, pepper, sugar and the wine vinegar. Put everything in a large pan and cook for 40 minutes until it thickens. Check for seasoning.

❹ Take the pan from the stove, pour the chutney into jars and seal tightly. Keep refrigerated and use within one week after opening.

Serves four, 860 kcal per serving.

Apple and mint jelly

This apple and mint jelly recipe is a true British classic. Little scones spread with it are delicious with afternoon tea.

1 kg/2¼ lb apples
1 bunch of mint
peel from 1 unsprayed lemon
1.75 litres/3 pints (8 cups) cider
1 kg/2¼ lb preserving sugar
brandy

❶ Wash the apples, remove the cores and quarter. Chop into large chunks. Put the apple chunks into a saucepan with the cider.

❷ Wash the mint, tie together with the lemon peel and add to the apples and cider in the pan. Add the preserving sugar and bring briefly to the boil. Add brandy to taste.

❸ Put the mint jelly in the refrigerator and leave it to cool.

Makes 1.5 kg/3 lb, about 60 kcal per serving.

Gourmet sauce

This delicious apple sauce with finely chopped almonds is also a wonderful condiment to go with cold cuts of meat and poultry dishes. It can be used instead of mayonnaise for making sandwiches, for example with turkey breast or pastrami.

❶ Peel, quarter and core the apples. Grate the apple quarters and put in a bowl. Add the lemon juice and mix thoroughly.

❷ Add the mayonnaise and almonds and mix well. Add salt and pepper to taste.

Serves four, 270 kcal per serving.

250 g/8 oz apples

juice of ½ lemon

100 g/3½ oz (scant ½ cup) mayonnaise

50 g/2 oz (½ cup) finely chopped almonds

salt

freshly ground white pepper

Devil's dip

This cold dip is a wonderful complement to cold meat or roast beef. You can adjust how hot and spicy it is by using more or less pepper. This sauce also goes well with sandwiches.

❶ Peel, quarter and core the apples. Cut the quarters into fine julienne strips.

❷ Put the apples in a bowl and add the tomato ketchup (catsup), mustard, mayonnaise and lemon juice. Stir well.

❸ Season with salt and pepper. Wash the chives, snip into little round sections and stir in. Serve the sauce hot or cold.

Serves four, 110 kcal per serving.

100 g/3½ oz apples

100 g/3½ oz (scant ½ cup) tomato ketchup (catsup)

20 g/¾ oz (2 tablespoons) mustard

40 g/1½ oz (4 tablespoons) mayonnaise

juice of ½ lemon

salt

freshly ground black pepper

½ bunch chives

Whipped apple cream

Whipped apple cream can be served with cakes and any dish where one would normally use whipped cream. The apple flavour makes this an exquisite substitute for whipped cream.

1 kg/2¼ lb apples
6 leaves of gelatine
250 g/8 oz (1 cup) sugar
½ sachet vanilla sugar

❶ Peel, quarter and core apples. Grate the apples finely.

❷ Dissolve the gelatine according to the instructions on the packet

❸ Put the apples in a bowl, add the sugar, vanilla sugar and the dissolved gelatine and beat until the consistency becomes foamy. Use in the same way as whipped cream, with cakes, apple sauce or apple purée.

Serves four, 410 kcal per serving.

Apple mayonnaise

Apple mayonnaise can be served separately as a sauce with various dishes, or it can be used as a substitute for normal mayonnaise. It is particularly good when used instead of normal mayonnaise in the traditional buffet dish egg mayonnaise with caviar.

❶ Peel, quarter and core the apples. Grate the quarters finely.

❷ Add lemon juice, mayonnaise and hazelnuts (filberts) to the apples. Stir together until the consistency becomes creamy.

❸ Add white wine to the cream shortly before serving and mix well.

Serves four, 170 kcal per serving.

250 g/8 oz apples

juice of ½ lemon

3 tablespoons mayonnaise

3 tablespoons roasted and grated hazelnuts (filberts)

20 ml/1 fl oz (2 tablespoons) white wine

Index

A

Alcohol 8

American upside-down cake 89

Apple amaretto tart 91

Apple and cabbage pie 54

Apple and cheese salad 31

Apple and chicken kebabs 27

Apple and curd (farmer's) cheese
  casserole 127

Apple and pork fillet (tenderloin)
  kebabs 51

Apple and fish dip with curry sticks 21

Apple and mint jelly 146

Apple and onion quiche 67

Apple and strawberry tartlets 109

Apple and tuna salad 38

Apple and vanilla ice cream 110

Apple and vegetable stew 63

Apple and walnut parfait 112

Apple and wine cream pie 95

Apple-beer punch 138

Apple and bilberry (blueberry) drink
  136

Apple beignets à la princesse 104

Apple cake
  – American upside-down 89
  – Hidden apple cake 90
  – Submerged apple cake 86

Apple Chelsea pastries 97

Apple chicken in puff pastry 57

Apple chutney 146

Apple compote
  – fresh 122
  – preserve 121
  – with raspberries 123

Apple confection 116

Apple crepes 68

Apple crumble 93

Apple dumplings 73

Apple fritters 100

Apple jam (jelly) 144

Apple juice 134

Apple kebabs 28

Apple Lindau 41

Apple magic 119

Apple mayonnaise 151

Apple milkshake 140

Apple pancakes (crepes) 68

Apple pastries 97

Apple-peel tea 132

Apple pizza 59

Apple preserve 121

Apple relish 145

Apple rings
  – fritters 100
  – with vanilla cream 126

Apple rings with vanilla cream 126

Apple salad
  – romantique 38
  – with herb liqueur 125
  – with herrings 37

Apple sauce 120

Apple sorbet 113

Apple sponge slices 101

Apple stories 10

Apple strudel 76

Apple surprise 118

Apple temptation with candied flower
  petals 115

Apple turnovers 98

Apple varieties
  – Ashmead Kernel 14
  – Bramley 16
  – Cox's Orange Pippin 14
  – Edward VII 16

  – Elstar 14
  – Golden Delicious 14
  – Jonagold 14
  – Russet 16
  – Orleans Reinette 16
  – Worcester 14

Apple vinegar drink 135

Apple water 135

Apple woodruff punch 139

Apples
  – baked in pastry 107
  – filled with game 65
  – in zabaglione 115
  – with custard 114
  – with fruit filling 119

B

Baked apples 128

Baked apples in pastry 107

Baked apple with sauerkraut filling
  55

Bean and apple hot-pot with smoked
  pork 70

Beignets à la Princesse 104

C

Casserole 60

Chicory with apples 36

Chilled apple and redcurrant soup 39

Chilled apple soup 114

Chutney, apple 146

Classic apple-mint jelly 146

Cooking (green) apples 16

Cream tart 95

Curry risotto with apple 63

D

Devil's dip 149

Drinks 132, 134, 135, 136, 140

Duck with apple and potato gratin 71

E
Eating apples 14
Eggs 8
Elderberry and apple Jam (jelly) 143

F
Fish dishes with
  – cod fillets 78
  – prawns (shrimps) 26
  – salted herring 20
  – smoked mackerel 21
  – squid 79
French apple tart 82
Fried grated potatoes with apples 25
Fruit salad 34

G
Game dishes
  – Hunter's apples 65
  – Pheasant à la Normande 44
  – Hare with apples 64
Ginger apples flambé 106
Glace aux pommes 113
Glazed apple tart 88
Gourmet sauce 147
Grated salad 29, 35
Gratin
  – Duck with apple and potato 71
  – Hamburger patties and apple 72
Guinea fowl with cider and apples
  56

H
Hamburger patties and apple gratin
  72
Hare with apples 64
Heavenly bed of apples 52
Herbs 8
Hidden apple cake 90
Hunters' apples 65

I
Ice cream
  – Apple and vanilla 110
  – Apple and walnut parfait 112

J
Jam (jelly)
  – Elderberry and apple jam (jelly) 143
  – Special apple jam (jelly) 144

L
Lamb pie with apples 48
Liver and apples 45

M
Mayonnaise, apple 151
Meat dishes with
  – fillet of beef 54
  – hamburger 28, 72
  – lamb 48
  – pork 60
  – pork chops 50
  – pork fillet (tenderloin) 47, 51
  – smoked pork 55, 70
Milk 8
Minerals 12

N
Nutrition 12
Nuts 8

P
Pancakes (crepes) 68
Pastry 54
Pheasant 44
Pitta bread with chicken and apple
  filling 22
Pizza 59
Pork casserole with apples 60
Pork chops with apple cream 50

Pork fillet (tenderloin) with apples 47
Poultry 8
Poultry dishes with apple
  – chicken 22, 27, 57
  – duck 71
  – guinea fowl 56
Power drink 140
Power salad 29
Prawn (shrimp) cocktail with apples
  26

Q
Quiche 67
Quick apple cake 85
Quick dishes
  – Apple and vegetable stew 63
  – Apple cake 85
  – Apple rngs with vanilla cream 126
  – Hidden apple cake 90
  – Pork chops with apple cream 50

R
Raspberry apple compote 123
Red cabbage with apples 62
Regional specialties
  – American 89
  – Asian 32
  – Austrian 75
  – English 146
  – French 82, 114
  – Mediterranean 22
  – northern German 20, 128
  – Russian 54
  – southern German 41, 76, 88
Relish, Apple 145
Rhubarb and apple pie 84
Rice pudding with apples 74
Rolled fish with apples and vegetables
  78
Rum and apple pie 94

S

Salad
- 1001 Nights 32
- Apple and cheese 31
- Apple and herring 37
- Apple and peach 125
- Apple and tuna 38
- Chicory and apple 36
- Fruit 34
- Romantique 38
- Waldorf 35

Sauce, cold 149

Sausage dishes
- pork 34

- smoked 52

Schwabian apple tart 88

Sherb 113

Shrimp cocktail with apples 26

Silly rascal 20

Sponge fingers 114

Squid kebabs with apple sauce 79

Submerged apple cake 86

Sweet pancakes (crepes) with apples 75

T

Tea 132

Tipsy apple and peach salad 125

V

Vegetable dishes
- Apple and onion quiche 67
- Apple dumplings 73
- Fried grated potatoes with apples 25
- Red cabbage with apples 62
- Rice pudding with apples 74

Vitamins 12

W

Waldorf Salad 35

Whipped apple cream 150

Produced by
Meidenbauer - Martin Verlagsbüro,
Munich, Germany
Layout and typesetting
Hubert Grafik Design, Munich,
Germany
Photography
Brigitte Sporrer and Alena Hrbkova
Food preparation
Tim Landsberg
Cover illustration
© Christel Rosenfeld
Cover design
BOROS, Wuppertal, Germany
Translation
Greta Dunn
Printed and bound by
Druckerei Appl, Wemding,
Germany

© 2000 DuMont Verlag, Cologne,
Germany
(monte von DuMont)
All rights reserved

ISBN 3-7701-7001-6

Printed in Germany

The recipes in this book have been
carefully researched and worked
out. However, neither the author
nor the publishers can be held li-
able for the contents of this book.

The editors and publishers would
like to give special thanks to the
following business for the support
of this book:

Culti
Munich, Germany: 46

The author
Martina Blank was born and grew
up in the USA. She now lives near
Tegernsee in southern Germany.
She is a free-lance author whose
main areas of interest are nutrition
and health.

The photographers
Brigitte Sporrer and Alena Hbrkova
met each other during their training as photographers in Munich,
Germany. After being assistants
to various advertising and food
photographers, they now each
have their own studios in Munich
and Prague respectively.

The food preparation
Tim Landsberg, who learned to
cook in Bonn, Germany, works in
Munich as a food stylist. His cus-
tomers are from the printing and
television advertising branches.
He also likes to work on cook-
books.

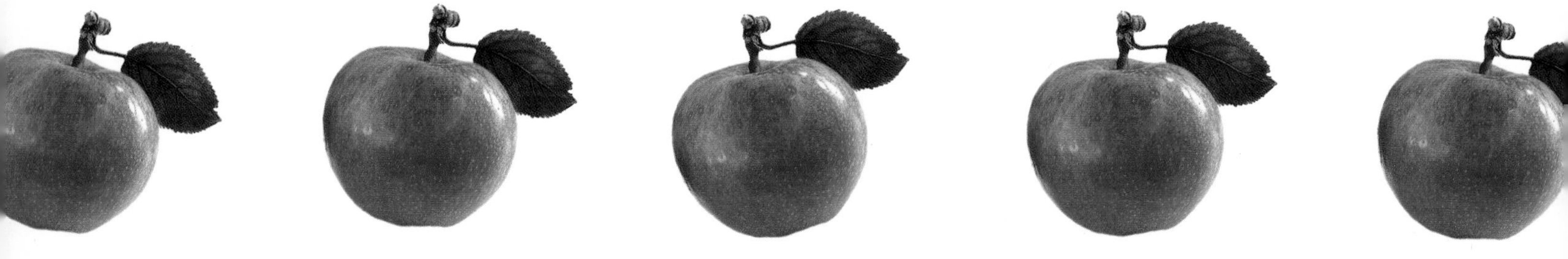